Proceedings of the Seventh International Workshop on
Digital Forensics & Incident Analysis (WDFIA 2012)

Crete, Greece
6-8 June 2012

Editors

Nathan Clarke
Theodore Tryfonas
Ronald Dodge

Centre for Security, Communications & Network Research
Plymouth University

ISBN: 978-1-84102-316-8

© 2012 Plymouth University
All rights reserved
Printed in the United Kingdom

No part of this book may be reproduced, stored in a retrieval system, or transmitted in any form or by any means – electronic, mechanical, photocopy, recording or otherwise, without the prior written permission of the publisher or distributor.

Preface

The field of digital forensics is rapidly evolving and continues to gain significance in both the law enforcement and the scientific community. Being intrinsically interdisciplinary, it draws upon a wide range of subject areas such as information & communication technologies, law, social sciences and business administration.

With this in mind, the workshop on Digital Forensics and Incident Analysis (WDFIA) specifically addresses this multi-facetted aspect, with papers invited from the full spectrum of issues relating to the theory and practice of digital forensics and incident analysis.

This book represents the proceedings from the 2012 event, which was held in Crete, Greece, co-located with IFIP SEC 2012. A total of 13 papers are included, spanning a range of topics including systems and network investigation, services and applications and supporting the forensic process. All of the papers were subject to double-blind peer review, with each being reviewed by at least two members of the international programme committee. This year the workshop also focused upon a special theme focussed upon forensic education and to this end collaborated with IFIP WG 11.8 on Information Security Education. Whilst this year, we didn't receive any papers in this area, it is an important area of research that future calls will also consider.

We would like to thank the authors for submitting their work and sharing their findings, and the international programme committee for their efforts in reviewing the submissions and ensuring the quality of the resulting event and proceedings. We would also like to thank Dimitris Gritzalis for acting as the local Chair. His support was invaluable in making this workshop a success.

Nathan Clarke, Theodore Tryfonas & Ronald Dodge
Editors, WDFIA 2012

Crete, June 2012

International Programme Committee

P. Bednar	University of Portsmouth	United Kingdom
S. Brenner	University of Dayton	USA
A. Cerezo	University of Malaga	Spain
C. Fuhrman	Ecole de technologie superieure	Canada
S. Furnell	Plymouth University	United Kingdom
J. Haggerty	Liverpool John Moores University	United Kingdom
C. Hargreaves	Cranfield University	United Kingdom
C. Hennell	British Telecom Openreach	United Kingdom
B. Hutchinson	Edith Cowan University	Australia
C. Illioudis	ATEI of Thessalonki	Greece
A. Irons	University of Sunderland	United Kingdom
A. Jones	Khalifa University	UAE
	Edith Cowan University	Australia
S. Karatzouni	University of Portsmouth	United Kingdom
M. Karyda	University of the Aegean	Greece
T. Karygiannis	National Institute of Standards and Technology (NIST)	USA
V. Katos	Democritus University of Thrace	Greece
G. Kessler	Champlain College	USA
S. Kokolakis	University of the Aegean	Greece
I. Kotenko	SPIIRAS	Russia
C.T. Li	University of Warwick	United Kingdom
T. Martin	Khalifa University	UAE
I. Mitchell	Middlesex University	United Kingdom
L. Mitrou	University of the Aegean	Greece
J. Niccolis	Avon & Somerset Police	United Kingdom
A. Patel	University of Kebangsaan	Malaysia
G. Pernul	University of Regensburg	Germany
G. Quirchmayr	University of Vienna	Austria
V. Roussev	University of New Orleans	USA
H. Tamman	Staffordshire University	United Kingdom
P. Thomas	University of Glamorgan	United Kingdom
C. Valli	Edith Cowan University	Australia

Contents

Forensic Profiling of an eBook Reader: An Example   1
M. Piccinelli and P. Gubian

Finding Digital Forensic Evidence in Graphic Design Applications   12
E.K. Mabuto and H.S Venter

Scalable Distributed Signature Detection   27
R. Hegarty, M. Merabti, Q. Shi and R. Askwith

On the Investigation of Application Specific Data within Digital Forensics   38
H. Baier and A. Brand

A Forensic Text Comparison in SMS Messages: A Likelihood Ratio Approach with Lexical Features   55
S. Ishihara

Forensic Analysis of User Interaction with Social Media: A Methodology   66
J. Haggerty, M.C. Casson, S. Haggerty and M.J. Taylor

Using Hypothesis Generation in Event Profiling for Digital Forensic Investigations   76
L. Pan, N. Khan and L. Batten

Pypette: A Framework for the Evaluation of Live Digital Forensic Acquisition Techniques   87
B. Lempereur, M. Merabti and Qi Shi

On Dimensions of Reconstruction in Database Forensics   97
O.M. Fasan and M.S. Olivier

Assessing Forensic Readiness   107
A. Chryssanthou and V. Katos

A Model for Hybrid Evidence Investigation   119
K. Vlachopoulos, E. Magkos and V. Chrissikopoulos

Towards Solving the Identity Challenge Faced by Digital Forensics   129
A. Valjarevic and H. Venter

Arguments and Methods for Database Data Model Forensics   139
H. Q. Beyers, M.S. Olivier and G.P. Hancke

Forensic Profiling Of An eBook Reader: An Example

M. Piccinelli and P. Gubian

Dept. of Information Engineering, Faculty of Engineering,
University of Brescia, Italy
email: mario.piccinelli@ing.unibs.it

Abstract

Forensics profiling refers to the study and exploitation of traces in order to draw a profile relevant to the investigation about criminal or litigious activities. While traces may not be strictly dedicated to a court use, they may increase knowledge of the subject under investigation. In this context we will study the evidence found in a modern ebook reader, and we will explain how it could be used during an investigation to help understand the profile and the habits of its owner by building a reliable timeline of all the interactions between the user and the device. We use as an example a modern ebook reader, the Sony Touch PRS-650, of which we present a complete profiling made with custom software.

Keywords

Ebook Reader, Forensics, Profiling.

1. Introduction

The aim of forensic research is to support investigatory and judicial processes by finding traces in otherwise apparently unpromising raw material from which it is possible to build a picture of events and activities (WP6, FIDIS Consortium, 2008). But digital evidence is not well perceived by human senses (Wang, 2007): crucial pieces of digital evidence may simply be overlooked due to the fact that examiners do not fully comprehend how seemingly useless pieces of data can be converted to evidence of high value (Koen R.). If, thanks to this apparently worthless information, an investigation team can understand an intruder's modus operandi, it might be possible to determine various attributes describing the intruder, such as skill level, knowledge and location (Casey, 2002). In this paper we decided to analyze an ebook reader. This kind of portable electronic device is seeing a notable growth, and it is becoming common for a forensics examiner to find such a device during an investigation. What we found during our research is that there is not a common methodology for the examination of this kind of device, mainly because readers contain a small amount of personal information regarding their owner and thus are deemed of little interest in an investigation. We will describe a new source of information: the time data that can be acquired from the logs of an ebook reader. This kind of evidence, which may be perceived as worthless, could in fact be helpful for acquiring additional information about the user of the device itself.

2. Ebook readers

Ebook readers are portable electronic devices designed primarily for the purpose of reading digital books. These devices, similar in form to tablet computers, are usually provided with hardware and software developed specifically for this single task. Each of these devices is considerably different from each other, in terms of hardware characteristics, connectivity (some models even ship with built-in WiFi connectivity) and data storage, and thus it is impossible to create a standard examination protocol. In this paper we will focus on a single model, the Sony Reader PRS-650.

2.1. Example: Sony Reader Touch PRS-650

The Reader Touch PRS-650 is a modern ebook reader manufactured by Sony. It uses an electronic paper display (6 inch, 16-level gray scale, 800x600 pixels), has a tablet form factor and is powered by a Lithium-ion rechargeable battery. The touch screen represents the main input; 5 buttons on the front face provide other input. It runs on MontaVista Linux and provides 2 GB of internal flash memory, which can be extended by a removable SDHC card and/or a removable Memory Stick PRO duo card. This ebook reader provides the capability of reading books in various formats and taking notes (handwritten on the touchscreen or typed into a simulated keyboard); it also provides instruments for saving bookmarks and drawing or highlighting words on each page of books (Sony Corporation, 2011). These capabilities will be explained in detail later as they will be the main sources of data for the profiling of the device.

3. Data Acquisition

Sony provides a client software named "Sony ebook library" to interact with the reader from a personal computer with Windows or Mac OS X operating systems. Nonetheless, the reader's storage can also be accessed without using specific software because the device itself is recognized, when connected to a PC via a standard USB cable, as a standard USB mass storage device. In detail, when the device is connected to a PC, it shows two to four single partitions:

1. a partition labeled "SETTING", formatted as MS-DOS FAT16, of 10.4 MB (of which 3.8 available) containing the installers for the Windows and Mac OS X versions of the Sony ebook library;

2. a partition labeled "READER", formatted as MS-DOS FAT32, of 1.61 GB containing the books stored in the internal memory of the device along with two folders, "database" and "Digital editions". The content of these two folders will be described later, as they contain the data we will use to build a profile of the user of the device;

3. if available, also the memory cards in the devices will be mounted as single partitions with their real volume name. These will contain, along with the

books stored in them, two folders named "Sony Reader" and "Digital Editions". Also these folders will be described later.

All the data contained in these volumes can easily be acquired and analyzed with standard forensically sound methods (see Carrier, 2005). It is noteworthy that this model isn't capable of wireless connectivity such as WiFi or 3G, which makes the forensics examination easier by rendering the device insulated from the outside world (and thus tamper proof) except for the USB connection, which can be write-protected by hardware or software means.

4. Data structure

As mentioned above, the analysis is based on the data found in specific folders in the internal storage of the reader and in the removable storage devices. During our research we found that the most interesting data are stored in the folders named *database* (on the internal storage) and *Sony Reader* (in the removable storage).

4.1. Sony Reader folder

The structure of a sample *Sony Reader* folder found in the SD card of the device under test is shown in Figure 1. The content of the single folders deemed useful for our analysis is described below.

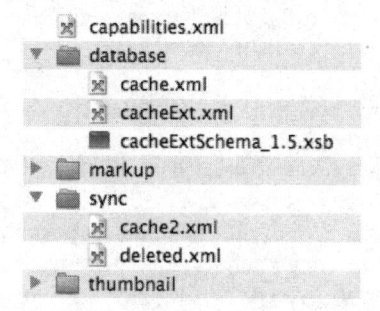

```
capabilities.xml
▼ database
    cache.xml
    cacheExt.xml
    cacheExtSchema_1.5.xsb
▶ markup
▼ sync
    cache2.xml
    deleted.xml
▶ thumbnail
```

Figure 1: *Sony Reader* **directory structure**

The file *capabilities.xml* stores information about the reader device: a list of the supported file types, a list of the supported markup elements, the display resolution and so on.

The folder *markup* contains the graphical files depicting the hands-free markups drawn on the eBooks by using the provided pen on the touchscreen. This directory mimics the directory tree of the SD card, each branch terminating with a last folder with the same name as the ebook it references. Each one of these low level folders contains the markup files for a single book. For each markup we found two files, with the same name (the unique id of the markup, as described later) but different extensions.

1. a JPG file, a compressed bitmap depicting a preview of the book page with the markup. Each JPG file weighs about 4 to 8 KB and has a resolution of approximately 110 x 150 pixels.

2. an SVG file, a vector graphics file depicting the markup drawing.

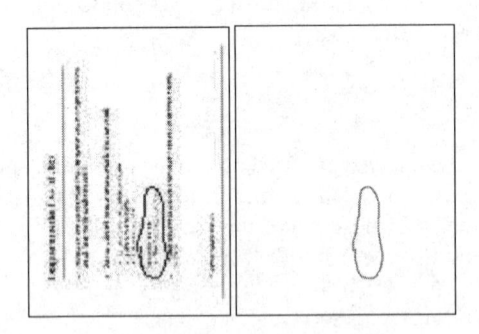

Figure 2: Example of hands free thumbnail and vector graphic

The folder *thumbnail* contains a directory structure similar to the one described for the *markup* folder. Each lowest level folder contains a single graphical file named *main_thumbnail.jpg* depicting a thumbnail representation of the book it references (usually the book cover).

The folder *cache* contains two XML files containing the main data used in our analysis, *cache.xml* and *cacheExt.xml*. The file *cache.xml* stores a list of all the books in the SD card. Each element of the list is saved as an XML node named "text", with attributes describing the document it refers to such as book title and author name, full path of the file relative to the root of the SD card, last page read and part (as the page can be zoomed and shown in more parts), a unique numerical id, MIME type of the file, date of creation, size in bytes. The file may also contain XML nodes named *playlist* describing lists of books; each node contains one child node for each book in the collection, identified by its unique id.

The file *cacheExt.xml* also stores a list of all the books in the SD card. Each element of the list is saved as an XML node named *text* with an attribute *path* containing the full path of the referred document relative to the root of the SD card. Each node may contain several child nodes:

1. *currentPosition*: a node depicting the position of the last read page of the document (page number and part) along with a timestamp. The node itself may contain a *mark* node depicting the current position in a support-dependent form, encoded in base64 format. For PDF files this position is represented as Adobe #pdfloc coordinates, (such as "#pdfloc(c81e,26)") while for epub files this position is represented as a link to a point in the

appropriate xhtml file inside the epub structure (such as "index_split_4.xhtml#point(/1/3/146/2/1/1:391)").

2. *preferences*: among the others, the user selected values of brightness and contrast. This node may also contain a child node of type *dicHistories*; each child of this node (of type *dicHistory*) is a recording for the action of looking up a word in one of the built-in dictionaries, which is achieved in the device under test by double clicking on the word while reading the document. Among the attributes of these bottom level nodes are the word looked up and the timestamp of the operation.

3. *thumbnail*: a node referring to the thumbnail image file for the book (specifying width and height), stored in the *thumbnails* folder seen above.

4. *history*: a node listing the last pages shown by the device (at most 100 entries). For each page seen, an *item* XML node is created with attributes describing, among other things, the page read (page number and part) and the timestamp. This node also contains two child nodes, *comment* and *mark*, containing the same information seen for the *currentPosition* node.

5. *markups* and *deletedMarkups*: these two nodes contain the markups and the deleted markups respectively for the document they refer to. These markups are stored as child nodes of three types: *annotation*, *freehand* and *bookmark2*. An annotation represents a piece of text that has been highlighted on the device; a freehand represents an annotation drawn on the device using the provided pen on the touchscreen; a bookmark represents a page (or a part of it) bookmarked. Each of these node types has different characteristics (for example, annotations store two child nodes named *start* and *end* pointing to the position of the selected text in support dependent format, as seen before for the *mark* nodes, while freehands also store child nodes pointing to the SVG file of the annotation and the thumbnail file of the page showing the drawing) but they all have some attributes in common, the most interesting of them being the position in the document (page number and part) and a timestamp (of creation for markups or deletion for the deleted ones) which will be used for building the timeline.

Notice that the child nodes of many of the nodes described before are related to an action performed by the user (moving to a page of a document, adding a bookmark, drawing a freehand note) and are provided with a timestamp, showing the date and time when the action was performed. These timestamps will be used later to build a timeline of the use of the device.

4.2. Database folder

The *database* folder found in the main storage (depicted in Figure 3) of the device corresponds the *Sony Reader* folder found on the SD card, with some remarkable exceptions.

The most easily detectable exceptions are that by default this folder also contains a subfolder named *media*, in which we found the multimedia files that came preloaded in the device and the files for the note application:

1. audio folder, containing some MP3 files;

2. books folder, containing some books in EPUB and RTF format;

3. images folder, containing some JPG images (by default they are used as screensavers);

4. notepads folder.

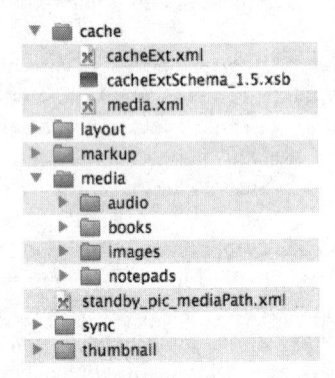

Figure 3: *Database* directory structure

The latter is the most useful one from a forensics perspective because it contains the files created by the note application. The note application lets the user create hands free notes (similar to the hands free markups which can be drawn on book pages), and stores them as single files in this folder with a *.note* extension. Each note file is in fact a vector graphic file, stored in an XML format similar to the SVG type, in which each line composing the drawing is described as a list of X/Y coordinates. The XML head of the file also contains a *note:notepad* attribute named *createDate*, which holds the creation date of the note file in Unix epoch format, which will be combined with other timing data to create a timeline of the device use.

Another difference between the *Sony Reader* folder described before and the *database* folder is that the latter contains, instead of the *cache.xml* file, another XML file named *media.xml* with a different structure. For documents, the *cache* nodes seen in *cache.xml* are replaced by *cache:text* nodes, holding the same information as seen before. Other node types are provided to support the different media types held in the device main storage:

1. *cache:notepad* nodes holding data about the .note files described before; among the attributes found in these nodes the most interesting are the creation timestamp and the full path of the .note file.

2. *cache:audio* nodes holding data about the MP3 files found on the device.

3. *cache:image* nodes holding data about the image files stored on the device.

4. Other node types deemed not useful for a forensics analysis: *cache:library*, *cache:watchSpecial*, *cache:playlist*.

All the aforementioned nodes are contained under a parent node named *records*.

An *cacheExt.xml* file was also found also in the *media* directory with a structure identical to what described for the *Sony Reader* directory. The only difference found is the presence of other node types different from *text*, used to describe documents; these nodes, whose types are *audio*, *image* and *notepad*, refer to the other media types described before but don't seem to hold forensically useful data.

5. Profiling with the data found

As we have shown in the previous section, during normal interaction between the user and the device a vast amount of data is created in the *Sony Reader* and *database* directories. This amount of data, stored as nodes in XML files, can be easily extracted from the device itself or an image of the device mass storage and attached cards created by standard forensically sound tools. During the extraction the data can also be easily protected from tampering, for example by producing an MD5 hash signature of each file upon extraction and checking it against an hash of the same files on the device.

During this research we focused on the temporal data. While all the content of the device and its attached storages can be useful during a forensics examination, standard forensics tools can analyze those elements. The most interesting evidence we found that is not common to other digital devices is the presence in the cache files of timestamps for each action performed on the device, such as:

1. last reading of a document;

2. creation date of a document (as held by the filesystem);

3. creation date of a note;

4. reading of a page of a document (at most the last 100 for each document);

5. creation and deletion of markups (bookmarks, free hand drawings and highlighting);

6. look up for words in the built in dictionaries.

With all this data we will be able to create a chronology of the use of the device. For this purpose we created a simple Python script, which parses all of the nodes described above to acquire their timestamp and then outputs them in chronological order.

All the timestamps found in the device are stored as strings in GMT timezone, like "Thu, 18 Aug 2011 19:49:30 GMT". Unfortunately, the effective timezone of the device is not stored in the files described before nor anywhere else in the readable partitions, and it can't even be seen on the device settings menu, as it is set when the device in synchronized with the Sony software and cannot be modified by the user. The only way we found to know the offset between the device time and the local time is to compare the creation dates of the files, as written in the file "*cache.xml*" and as provided by the filesystem. This method, though, hasn't proven always reliable, especially if the device was frequently updated by adding files from different host computers and different applications, because even third-party software such as *Calibre* can't reliably identify the timezone setting of the device. A way to have these elements cleaned is by inserting in the device a clean SD card with just one file in it, and let the reader create its "*cache.xml*" file which will contain a timestamp to check against the real creation time of the file itself. This way the investigator has all means to know the real timezone of the device and the difference in time between the device itself and the reference time.

5.1. Analysis of sample data

To study the amount of data created during normal use of the device, we proceeded by creating simple interactions with a brand new document we uploaded for this purpose; after each interaction we extracted the XML files from the device and analyzed them.

We uploaded the test file (test.pdf) on the SD card by connecting the device with a personal computer with Mac Os X 10.6 Snow Leopard and copying it to the mounted volume corresponding to the card itself. After that we disconnected the device and let it restart (the device, when disconnected from the host computer, analyzes all its stored documents and updates the configuration files). Then we ran our utility and saw that the only element found by searching for the file name is the record in *cache.xml* with the creation date of the document, which is equivalent to the creation date of the file as seen by the host computer filesystem.

```
2008-12-22 17:28:04    Creation date of test.pdf
```

After that we just opened the book (without browsing any page) and repeated the analysis. This time the device added to the *cache.xml* file the current position (page 0) and added to *cacheExt.xml* a history element depicting the reading of page 0.

```
2011-09-29 13:18:24    Current position page 0 of 291 of test.pdf
2011-09-29 13:18:24    Reading page 0 of 291 of test.pdf
```

The next step was browsing through the first pages of the book, and repeating the analysis. This time the device had correctly recorded as history elements all the pages we opened in the rightful sequence. It is interesting to note that the first time the cover page was opened it was recorded as a 0 page, while after turning to the next page it saved two records, one for the second page (as expected) and one for the first page (with the same timestamp). Also, the current position data was updated with the new timestamp and new page number.

```
2011-09-29 13:18:24    Reading page 0 of 291 (offset 0) of test.pdf
2011-09-29 13:20:13    Reading page 2 of 291 (offset 0) of test.pdf
[...]
2011-09-29 13:20:37    Reading page 9 of 291 (offset 0) of test.pdf
2011-09-29 13:20:39    Current position page 9 of 291 of test.pdf
```

After that we created some markups: a bookmark, a free hand drawing and a highlighting. The analysis correctly reported all these operations. Also, the file *cache.xml* was updated with a bookmark record with the timestamp of the last markup annotation.

```
2011-09-29 13:22:26    Bookmark2 markup at page 9 of 291 of test.pdf
2011-09-29 13:22:59    Freehand markup (1317302575979.063.svg) at page
        9 of 291 of test.pdf
2011-09-29 13:23:18    Bookmark date of book ottimismo.pdf
2011-09-29 13:23:18    Annotation ("ont") at page 9 of 291 of test.pdf
```

At last, we proceeded with deleting the markups and creating some new bookmarks, to see how the system managed the deleted markups. As we can see, the entries for the markups described before were deleted, and new entries were added under the *deletedMarkups* node in *cacheExt.xml*, with the timestamp of the deletion date (this means that we lost the creation date of the markups during the process).

```
2011-09-29 13:26:46    Deleted Bookmark2 at page 9 of 291 of test.pdf
2011-09-29 13:27:23    Deleted Annotation at page 9 of 291 of test.pdf
2011-09-29 13:27:36    Deleted Freehand at page 9 of 291 of test.pdf
[...]
2011-09-29 13:28:23    Bookmark2 markup at page 12 of 291 of test.pdf
2011-09-29 13:29:08    Bookmark2 markup at page 13 of 291 of test.pdf
2011-09-29 13:29:09    Bookmark date of test.pdf
2011-09-29 13:29:25    Current position page 13 of 291 of test.pdf
```

With the results from this last test we built a custom script to create a graph with the usage data of the device (Figure 4), limited to the useful selected time span and excluding the file creation date (which is not related to an interaction between the user and the device and could be misleading). In the graph, each line represents an interaction (we didn't find useful to discriminate among different kinds of interaction). This way we can easily understand how the device was used during this time.

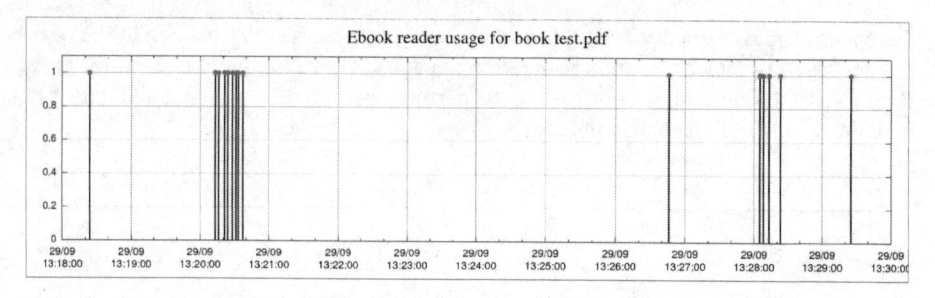

Figure 4: Usage data related to the test described before

We also performed other more general tests on the device, and obtained some more useful usage graphs related to a longer time span. For example, Figure 5 shows the usage of the device in a two months time span. In this graph we chose to differentiate among interactions regarding different books, by assigning each book a different value on the Y-axis. This way we can also see whether the user accessed many times the same book or instead briefly accessed many different documents.

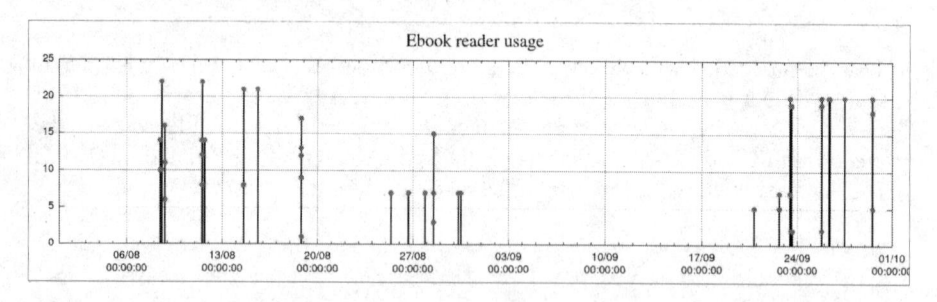

Figure 5: Usage data related to a 2 months timespan (august-september 2011)

6. Conclusions

The analysis performed on the device confirmed that it is possible to extract a forensically sound timeline of the usage of the device itself, and this timeline proved to be accurate at the single second. Virtually each operation performed by the user is logged and can be added to the timeline. During an investigation the timeline can be associated with a suspected, provided that investigators can prove that the device has always been in the exclusive availability of a single person. The evidence gathered this way could then be used in court to draw a behavioral profile of a suspected offender, support or deny an alibi, or provide additional useful information about the owner of the device.

7. About the software

The software used during this analysis was written by the authors and named "Sony Ebook Reader Time Profiler". It is a Python script and works from the command line, without graphical interface. When the application is launched, it scans the provided path/paths searching for files named *media.xml*, *cache.xml* or *cacheExt.xml*, and parses each one searching for timestamp data. This data is then ordered and printed on the console. Additionally the software can also build a data file that can then be fed to a provided GnuPlot script to create a timeline graph.

The code has been released under an open source license and is available at the following URL: *https://github.com/PicciMario/Sony-Ebook-Reader-Time-Profiler/*.

We encourage interested people to try the software and maybe participate to the development by providing suggestions or code to handle different devices or reporting bugs.

8. References

Wang, S.-J. "Measures of retaining digital evidence to prosecute computer-based cyber-crimes." *Comput. Stand. Interfaces* 29, no. 2 (2007): 216-223.

WP6, FIDIS Consortium. *D6.7c: Forensics Profiling.* FIDIS Consortium, 2008.

Casey, E. "Uncertainty, and loss in digital evidence." *International Journal of Digital Evidence* 1, no. 2 (2002).

Carrier, B. *File System Forensic Analysis.* Addison Wesley Professional, 2005.

Koen R., Olivier M. S. "The use of file timestamps in digital forensics." ICSA, University of Pretoria, South-Africa.

Sony Corporation. *Sony Ebook reader PRS 650.* 2011. http://www.sony.co.uk/product/rd-reader-ebook/prs-650 (accessed 2011).

Finding Digital Forensic Evidence in Graphic Design Applications

E.K. Mabuto and H.S Venter

Department of Computer Science, University of Pretoria, Pretoria, South Africa
e-mail: emabutos@cs.up.ac.za, hsventer@cs.up.ac.za

Abstract

Graphic design applications are often used for the editing and design of digital art. The same applications can be used for creating counterfeit documents like identity documents (IDs), driver's licenses or passports among others. However the use of any graphic design application leaves behind traces of digital information which can be used during a digital forensic investigation. Current digital forensic tools examine a system to find digital evidence but they do not examine a system specifically for the creating of counterfeit documents. This paper reviews the digital forensics analysis process involved in the creation of counterfeit documents by determining and corroborating the events that previously occurred. The analysis is achieved by associating the digital forensic information gathered to the possible actions taken, precisely, the scanning, editing, saving and printing of counterfeit documents. The digital forensic information is gathered by analyzing the files generated by the particular graphic design application used for document creating. Another analysis is conducted on user generated files, the actual files that can be used as potential evidence to establish file structural contents and the relationship with the associated actions. This involves analyzing the user generated files associated with these applications and determining their signatures and related metadata. Contextually, the authors illustrate an evaluation disclosing the digital forensic evidence gathered from graphic design applications.

Keywords

Digital evidence, Digital forensics, Digital forensic artifacts, Graphic design applications

1 Introduction

A great number of professions and industries such as advertising, newspaper printing, architecture, fashion and design, project management and manufacturing, depend upon being able to create complex graphic designs in the course of their work. It is for this reason that graphic design applications have numerous image-enhancing tools such as paint brushing, vector drawing, digital pen and pencil drawing and many others. Such graphic design applications use computer-aided design to create unique art for company logos, magazine advertisements and many other purposes. There are numerous individuals who rely upon being able to use graphic design applications to create visual presentations that utilize pictorial images to communicate and express ideas.

In another related development, the use of forged documents has become ubiquitous all over the world. Ilham Rawoot observes, in an article in the "Mail and Guardian" that terrorists make particular use of forged South African passports because of the ease with which these can be faked (Mail and Guardian Website, (2011)). But counterfeit documents are in circulation all over the world. The same graphic design applications that are used by professionals in their work can also be used for illegitimate purposes such as creating counterfeit documents. The problem is that, with the editing and design capabilities of these graphic design applications, they can be used to create extremely convincing counterfeit documents such as IDs, passports and drivers licenses. Criminal activities such as these necessitate the need for digital forensic investigations.

The use of graphic design applications leaves behind traces that can be revealed during a digital forensic investigation. A digital forensic investigation generally consists of the following phases: the acquisition, examination, analysis and reporting (U.S National Institute of Justice, 2001). Wherever an individual is suspected of creating counterfeit documents, the regular process of acquisition is followed. Generally the phases of acquisition and reporting are similar in different cases; therefore focus is on the examination and analysis phases. The focus is also on determining what the examiner needs to know prior to examining digital evidence. This paper identifies and discusses the digital traces that are left behind after a counterfeiter has used graphic design applications. This is achieved by associating the actions taken during document creation to the traces left behind. In addition, a file analysis of files generated by a user from within the application is conducted. To address the problem, the authors focus on the following two steps. First, identify the digital forensic information that shows whether a document was scanned, edited, saved and printed. Digital forensic information can be found in graphic design applications where the source of the evidence is mainly system-generated. The second step entails identifying the contents of user- generated files by looking at the file signatures and related metadata. In so doing, over above these two steps, an association with the potential criminal may be achieved. However, it is not the focus of this paper to link the crime to an actual person.

The remainder of the paper is structured as follows. In the second section, some background about digital forensics is presented, and this is followed by a brief survey of graphic design applications. The third section, which is the contributing section, is divided into two parts. The first part highlights the potential evidence that the authors refer to as "digital forensic artifacts". The source of potential evidence referred to above equates to the results from actions taken. More precisely the actions involved could be document scanning, editing, saving and printing. Most of this would originate from the system registry and application log files. The second part is an examination of user-generated files. The source of potential evidence referred to in this part involves results from content identification and content examination of files utilized by graphic design applications. The authors also name the tools that can be used in aiding the analysis where applicable. The fourth section contains an evaluation of the kind of evidence that may be extracted from the graphic design applications. The fifth section concludes the paper.

2 Background

In the following section the authors provide some brief background literature on digital forensics including an explanation of digital evidence. The authors also define what is meant by digital forensic artifacts. The second section of the background consists of a very brief literature survey on graphic design applications.

2.1 Digital Forensics

At the Digital Forensics Research Workshop (DFRWS) in 2001, digital forensics was defined as the use of scientifically derived and proven methods toward the preservation, collection, validation, identification, analysis, interpretation, documentation and presentation of digital evidence derived from digital sources for the purpose of facilitating or furthering the reconstruction of events found to be criminal, or helping to anticipate unauthorized actions shown to be disruptive to planned operations.

The goal of a digital forensic investigation on a system is to find out what happened and who was responsible for a particular incident or crime. Digital forensic investigations focus on finding digital evidence after a computer or network security incident has occurred or locating data from systems that may form part of some litigation, even if it has been deleted. In this context, evidence is the most critical in any case. Therefore any items that can be considered to be of evidential value should be identified and collected (Jones and Valli, 2008).

2.1.1 Digital Evidence

Computer evidence or digital evidence is defined as any hardware, software or any data that can be used to prove one or more of the "who, what, when, where, why and how" questions of a security incident (Solomon et al., 2005). Computer evidence furthermore consists of digital files and their contents left behind after an incident. Casey defined digital evidence as any data that can be used to establish that a crime was committed or can prove a link between a crime and its victim or an offender (Casey, 2000). Digital evidence consists entirely of sequences of binary values called bits (Cohan, 2010). Traces that are left behind from the use of an application or from an operating system can be referred to as digital forensic artifacts.

2.1.2 Digital Forensic Artifacts

An examiner reveals the truth of an event by discovering and exposing the remnants of the event that have been left on the system. These remnants are known as artifacts, which can be referred to as digital evidence (Altheide and Carvey, 2011)However, due to the loaded legal connotations binding the term "evidence" the term "artifacts" is used more often. Evidence is referred to as something to be used during a legal proceeding. Artifacts are traces left behind due to activities and events, which may or may not be innocuous. The scattered evidence inside a system can indicate what has happened for a particular digital forensic investigation. Application artifacts left by installed applications can be an excellent source of potential evidence when performing an analysis. Also an artifact does not become evidence unless its ability to prove a fact has been established (Zelkowitz , 2009). Therefore it is necessary to reconstruct events that occurred by gathering all the possible digital information from a system.

In an investigation, how and where evidence is located differs depending on the crime being investigated, the platform (operating systems) and the application used to commit the crime.

2.2 Graphic design applications

Although many graphic design applications are currently available to users, Adobe Systems Incorporated is regarded as the largest software maker in the graphic design software category (Wall-street Journal Website, 2011). For the purposes of this research, the authors therefore undertook a case study by investigating Adobe graphic design applications. Adobe Photoshop, Adobe In-Design and Adobe Illustrator are Adobe applications that are used for graphic design purposes. Any one of these applications can be used for the editing of a document. It is therefore necessary to conduct an exclusive examination of the potential digital forensic evidence produced by these applications. Since most graphic design users prefer to use the latest editions, the authors used the latest version of Adobe (Version, CS5) in the experiments. It should be noted, however, that additional experiments with the two previous versions (CS4 and CS3) produced similar results. Any slight differences that are attributed to different versions will be mentioned wherever necessary throughout the paper.

3 Digital forensic evidence in graphic design applications

The authors created dummy counterfeit documents by using Adobe graphic design applications, and carried out various experiments in order to search for pertinent evidence left behind from the use of these graphic design applications. The contribution is divided in two parts. The first part highlights digital forensic artifacts found in graphic design applications where the source of the potential evidence is mainly system-generated with results mostly from registry entries and application log files. The second part of the experiments, which involves examination of user-generated files, highlights results from file content identification and examination.

Software reviews from 2011 revealed that the Windows operating system is still the most popular operating system (Gartner Research, 2011). The authors therefore conducted the analysis for forensic artifacts on a Windows 7 platform. For future work, focus can also be placed on other popular operating systems like Linux and Mac OS.

To respond to the problem stated earlier, that graphic design applications can be used for creating counterfeit documents, firstly four possible actions taken during the creation of a document were used as a hypothesis to gather digital forensic information related to graphic design applications. These actions are document scanning, document editing, document saving and document printing. The analysis is formulated to find the digital forensic information that indicates that these actions were actually taken. By following the actions taken an investigator is able to conduct an investigation in a uniform manner that helps to acquire the actual images like a human face used to create the document and the created counterfeit document. For example, if the document was scanned, then probably it was then edited. If not scanned then probably it was edited by acquiring a copy of the original from another source. If not edited then probably it was printed only after being edited from another source. If none of the four actions were taken then there is no need to ascertain whether or not the application was used in the creation of the document.

Furthermore to respond to the same problem, a user-generated file analysis section follows, with two sub-sections dealing with content identification and content examination.

Experimental results gleaned from finding the four actions are elaborated in the each of the subsections to follow.

3.1 System-generated digital forensic artifacts

"System-generated digital forensic artifacts" refer to those artifacts created by the application without user intervention, while "user-generated digital forensic artifacts refer" to artifacts created by the user intentionally. The latter are discussed later in the paper.

For the experiments conducted, the following section describes the techniques used on Adobe graphic design applications. Four sub-sections follow in this section, namely artifacts related to document scanning, editing, saving and printing. It should be noted, however, that not all applications have the same capabilities to perform all these actions. Therefore, not all actions are described for each graphic design application. However, initiation of one of the actions can lead to possible identification of potential evidence relating to the creation of counterfeit documents. The authors explain the artifacts gathered from each action precisely for each graphic design application. Adobe Illustrator does not record any information regarding the four actions in any of its log files. Therefore, for Adobe Illustrator essential information will be acquired from the exclusive examination of user-generated files still to follow in section 3.2.

3.1.1   Artifacts relating to document scanning

Generally, if one is to attempt to create a fraudulent document, one has to acquire an original document so as to imitate or copy it. Scanning is an option which results in a copy of the original document being available on pc for digital editing. Many different models of scanners are available, using various software packages for executing scan commands. Therefore, for this research, focus is on commands generated from within the graphic design application used for editing the scanned document, rather than determining if a document is a scanned document.

Out of the three graphic design applications under consideration, only Adobe Photoshop has the capability of scanning a document using the "import WIA support" document menu option. "Import WIA support" is a function that Adobe Photoshop uses to connect to available printers or scanners. The document scanned is loaded into a destination folder as prompted. The application then creates a folder, saves the scanned image, and opens the scanned image in the application.

After a document is scanned the application records the entry into one of its log files under the name of *Adobe Photoshop CSX Prefs.psp* located in *C:\Users\<username>\ AppData\ Roaming \Adobe\Adobe Photoshop CSX\Adobe Photoshop CSX Settings*. The *X* in *CSX* represents the particular Adobe version in use. This may be either version 3, 4, or 5. After analyzing the log file's binary data an entry with the location of the scanned file is located usually about mid section of the file size. For example, if the file is 165kb the scanned file information will be located at hex byte offset 0x17004. After analyzing the content at this hex location, the folder locations of all the scanned documents can be found there.

The regular process followed by a potential criminal is to edit the acquired document in order to falsify some of its content.

3.1.2   Artifacts relating to document editing

Document editing is one of the critical stages of creating a counterfeit document as it allows one to place or import objects of interest, for example a human face, a bar code or a fingerprint. These objects can be inserted onto the scanned document. In relation to the inserted documents or files, experiments were executed to establish what can be found from a system that indicates to the examiner what was inserted and from which location it was inserted from. All three graphic design applications in question have the capacity to edit a document through attaching or placing an image. The terms "attaching" or "placing" an image is seen as the same action, used interchangely in various applications. In this paper, the term "attaching" is used from here on. Attaching is one of the main functions that is used in graphic design applications.

3.1.2.1 Editing in Adobe Photoshop

The same log file mentioned earlier *(Adobe Photoshop CSX Prefs)* contains information with the name of the attached file and the location from which it was attached usually at a byte offset of about 0x17F40. With this information the authors managed to establish the names and location of attached documents. Furthermore, by looking at the stated location the actual image with the human face or fingerprint was found.

3.1.2.2 Editing in Adobe Indesign

A file named *InDesign SavedData* without a file extension is located in the located in the folder *C:\Users\ <username>\ AppData\Local\Adobe\InDesign\Version 5.0\Cache*. It contains information indicating the name of the attached file and the location from which it was attached usually in the beginning of the file.

3.1.3 Artifacts relating to document saving

Once a document has been edited, usually a user (or potential criminal) might need to save it, either for printing or further editing. In this section the authors look at what is found in the system that relates to saved documents. This information is vital as it can point to an examiner where a file was saved to. If deleted or moved, search commands can be executed based on the names of the files saved. This is done by specifying the name of the file when searching thereby reducing time spent during an investigation. All three applications under consideration have the capability to save edited documents in various file types. An exclusive examination on each of the file types created from saving actions is explained in section 3.2.

3.1.3.1 Saving in Adobe Photoshop

The same log file *(Adobe Photoshop CSX Prefs)* contains information about save entries. The file contains information about the name of the saved file, the location in which it was filed, and type of the file, located at mid offset of the file after the entries for attached files. The names are arranged in order of the last saved file first. This information about saved locations can be verified or compared to the registry entries. Values for the visited directories are acquired from the registry key, *HKEY_CURRENT_USER\Software\Adobe\Photoshop\ 11.0\VisitedDirs*.

3.1.3.2 Saving in Adobe Indesign

The same log file *(InDesign SavedData)* that was earlier mentioned in connection with editing actions, contains information about the name of the file saved, type of the file and the location saved to. This information is located from mid offset of the file with the last saved file first. This information is located up to the end of the file depending on the number of documents saved.

Generally, saved files from any graphic design application can be verified or checked also by looking at the recent documents accessed from *C:\Users\<username>\ AppData\Roaming\Microsoft\Windows\Recent*.

3.1.4 Artifacts relating to document printing

Printing is one if not the last stages of potential counterfeit document creation. A user might need to create the hard copy of the edited document so that it can be used in a physical environment. Unlike scanning actions, printing actions can be commanded from all the graphic design applications under consideration via the menu command: print.

To locate which printer(s) are used to generally print a document one uses the registry. The keys from which a list of printers connections could be established from are

(1) *HKLM\soft\Adobe\Photoshop\11.0\Plugin* path.
(2) *HKEY_CURRENT_CONFIG\System\CurrentControlSet\Control\Print\Printers*
(3) *HKEY_USERS\<user id>\Software\Microsoft\Windows NT\CurrentVersion\PrinterPorts*
(4) HKEY_USERS\<userid>\Software\Microsoft\Installer\Products\41E0A130314079C4792762937B284FF6\ SourceList

After the names of the printers have been established, an investigator can verify the physical existence of the printer. This helps an investigator usually in cases where the printers have been physically removed. Moreover, given that the option to keep printed documents was enabled in the printers' properties before printing a counterfeit document. For each print job there are two spool files generated by the operating system located in *C:\Windows\System32\spool\ PRINTERS*. The first is *XXX.shd* and *XXX.spl* where *XXX* represents the job number. Analyzing the binary data of these files indicates the name of the printed document in the beginning of the **.spl* file. Towards the end of the **.shd* file is the name of the printed file, the location from which it was printed from and the name of the printer used to print the document. The timestamp of the **.spl* and **.shd* file indicates the date and time the document was created. This information is vital in establishing which counterfeit documents were actually printed.

Once the names and locations of the files have been established, an investigator needs to examine the actual identified files. These are the files that can be used as potential evidence in legal proceedings. This process is described in the following section.

3.2 User-generated artifacts from file examination

In order to conduct an exclusive examination on a crime conducted within an application the digital forensic examiner has to understand the nature of the files that are generated from that particular application, in this case, graphic design applications. This is so that the examiners are able to uncover and exploit any digital forensic artifacts present in the identified files (Altheide and Carvey, 2011).

As previously stated, user-generated digital forensic artifacts refers to files created by the user intentionally. User generated file artifacts can be divided into two distinct categories, which are, content identification and content examination. Content identification is the process of determining or verifying the type of a specific file. Content examination is the retrieval of any embedded metadata that may be present in a given file.

In the case of the examination of counterfeit documents the digital forensic examiner might need to identify potential changes inside files consistently, for example, the involvement of a fingerprints, barcodes or human faces embedded inside graphic design application file formats. The four graphic design applications discussed above are associated with more than thirty nine file types. However, for this research the authors focus was only on file types that are specific to the three graphic design applications, thus ignoring well-known file types like jpeg, bitmap, tag, tiff, tga etc. Gary Kesler and Martin Reddy keep a list of these common file signatures online, which is a continuing work in progress database (Kesler and Reddy, 2011)).

3.2.1 Content identification

As already been stated, content identification involves verifying the identity of a file extension. An offender can alter the file extension of a particular file in order to promote ambiguity. Therefore there is need to identify a files integrity by file signature analysis. An examiner needs to know what a particular file type is. A file is normally analyzed within its first bytes to determine the specific signature (Carvey, 2009). The file signature is therefore located at specific offsets usually in the beginning of a file.

It can be noted from the research conducted that known digital forensic tools like FTK can detect various file types but not for graphic design applications discussed in this paper. For example, digital forensic tools can verify file types like tga, bmp, gif, tif and png amongst others, but not the file types of graphic design applications as discussed in this paper.

The analysis to determine a graphic design file signature was also conducted using a hex editor. These values are generally hexadecimal values. Table 1 contains the list of file signatures identified and specific to the graphic design applications previously discussed. The file type in Table 1 represents the named form of the particular graphic design file. Proof of the real file identity resides within the content of the file, usually known as the file signature. The file extension is merely a suffix that represents the encoding of a file's content, usually three or four characters separated by a dot from the file name. However, the file extension should never be trusted as it can be renamed to anything else. One should rather focus on the file signature to determine the correct file type. The ASCII column in Table 1 represents the entry in text-readable format. The file signature columns represent the entry in hexadecimal format. Both these entries appear exactly as shown in the hex editor. The digital forensic examiner can use the information in Table 1 to identify the particular files for the graphic design applications in question.

File Type	File extension	ASCII	File signature
Illustrator file	ai	%PDF-1.5	25 30 44 46 2D 31 2E 35
Photoshop	psd	8BPS..	38 42 50 53 00 01
Indesign markup	idml	PK.......	50 4B 03 04 14 00 00 00
Indesign interexchange	incx	<?xml version="1.0"	3C 3F 78 6D 6C 20 76 65 72 73 69 6F 6E 3D 22 31 2E 30 22
Illustrator Postscript	eps	ADOE	C5 D0 D3 C6
Photoshop dcs2	eps	ADOE	C5 D0 D3 C6
Indesign document	indd	....	06 06 ED F5 D8 4D 46 E5 BD 31 EF E7 FE 74 B7 1D 44 4F 43 55
Indesign template	indt	....	06 06 ED F5 D8 4D 46 E5 BD 31 EF E7 FE 74 B7 1D 44 4F 43 55
Illustrator template	ait	%PDF-1.5	25 30 44 46 2D 31 2E 35

Table 1: Graphic design file signatures

3.2.2 Content Examination

Content examination involves determining the metadata of files, in this case, graphic design application file types. Metadata refers to data about data (C.Altheide, H.Carvey, 2011). On Windows systems this includes modified, accessed, creation times only to mention a few. The same hex editors, as previously stated, are used to examine the content of files associated with graphic design applications. Metadata is essential during an investigation as this reveals what useful information can be extracted from a particular file, for example this can be time stamps or name of the user who created the file.

Table 2 shows the metadata acquired from graphic design file types. The offset is the address pointer of the described metadata. In other words, if an examiner searched for a certain offset, the hex editor would skip to the particular metadata. Several experiments however revealed that the offset can vary slightly by plus or minus 780 bytes per metadata, which is usually in the same page view depending on the size of the file and quantity of metadata present in the file. Therefore the tabulated values can still be used on graphic design files of different sizes. The metadata is embedded in Extensible Metadata Platform (xmp) tags, which is Adobe's way of embedding metadata in its various file types (Adobe XMP, 2011).

File type	File extension	Description of Metadata	Offset (Address pointer to Metadata)	Example of the Metadata (As presented in a hex editor)
Indesign document	indd	File location for any imported image files	D9EB	file:C:/Users/<username>/Pictures/ dvd%20picture%20sleeves/Capture_005% 20%282%29.JPG
		Name of application that created the file	E510B or E6E16	<stEvt:softwareAgent>Adobe InDesign 6.0</stEvt:softwareAgent>
		String events of saving history	F0D0C to F12FE	<stEvt:action>created</stEvt:action> <stEvt:when>2011-05-04T15:13:25+02:00</stEvt:when><stEvt:action>saved</stEvt:action><stEvt:when>2011-05-04T15:15:43+02:00</stEvt:when>
		Date file was created	F5263	CreateDate>2011-05-04T15:13:25+02:00
		Metadata Date	F52A7	MetadataDate>2011-05-04T15:18:24+02:00</xmp:MetadataDate
		Modify Date	FD2EA	<xmp:ModifyDate>2011-05-04T15:18:24+02:00</xmp:ModifyDate>
Illustrator Postscript file	eps	Name of application that created the file	57	%%Creator: Adobe Illustrator(R) 14.0
		Date file was created	8E	%%CreationDate: 9/17/2011
		Login name of user that created the file	73	%%For: <username>\ %
Illustrator file	ai	Metadata Date	3A7	<xmp:MetadataDate>2011-05-04T15:51:17+02:00</xmp:MetadataDate>
		Date file was modified	3ED	<xmp:ModifyDate>2011-05-04T15:51:17+02:00</xmp:ModifyDate>
		Date file was created	431	<xmp:CreateDate>2011-05-04T15:51:17+02:00</xmp:CreateDate>
		Name of application that created the file	476	<xmp:CreatorTool>Adobe Illustrator CSX</xmp:CreatorTool>
Photoshop file	psd	Name of application that created the file	1A9	<xmp:CreatorTool>Adobe Photoshop CSX Windows</xmp:CreatorTool>
		Date file was created	1F0	<xmp:CreateDate>2011-05-04T14:39:08+02:00</xmp:CreateDate>
		Date file was modified	234	<xmp:ModifyDate>2011-05-04T14:50:23+02:00</xmp:ModifyDate>
		Metadata date	27A	<xmp:MetadataDate>2011-05-04T14:50:23+02:00</xmp:MetadataDate>
		String events of saving history	6FF to 717	<stEvt:instanceID>xmp.iid:DE0657134D76E011B00EFDC555D228CB</stEvt:instanceID> <stEvt:when>2011-05-04T14:50:23+02:00</stEvt:when>
Illustrator template	ait	Name of application that created the file	1F3 or 452	<xmp:CreatorTool>Adobe Illustrator CSX</xmp:CreatorTool>
		Metadata Date	383	<xmp:MetadataDate>2011-05-04T15:51:17+02:00</xmp:MetadataDate>
		Date file was modified	3C9 or 16323	<xmp:ModifyDate>2011-05-04T15:51:17+02:00</xmp:ModifyDate>
		Date file was created	40D	<xmp:CreateDate>2011-05-04T15:51:17+02:00</xmp:CreateDate>
		String events of saving history	D02B or D5D3	<stEvt:action>saved</stEvt:action> <stEvt:instanceID>xmp.iid:FF7F117407206811B628E3BF27C8C41B</stEvt:instanceID> <stEvt:when>2011-05-22T16:23:53-07:00</stEvt:when>
		Name of user that created the file	17FB9	%%For: (Pinchers) ()
		File path for any imported images	D727	%%DocumentFiles:C:\Users\<username>\Pictures\Sizzla-Soul Deep-Front.jpg %%+C:\Users\<username>\\Pictures\Tulips.jpg
		List of previous files names used	180A8	/Title(illustrator .ait template)
Indesign interexchange file	incx	Date file was created	BFD3	<xmp:CreatorTool>Adobe InDesign 6.0</xmp:CreatorTool>
		Metadata Date	C019	<xmp:MetadataDate>2011-05-04T15:17:21+02:00</xmp:MetadataDate>
		Date file was modified	C05F	<xmp:ModifyDate>2011-05-04T15:17:21+02:00</xmp:ModifyDate>

		Date file was created	BD3A	<xmp:CreateDate>2011-05-04T15:17:21+02:00</xmp:CreateDate>
		Name of application that created the file	C0A4	<xmp:CreatorTool>Adobe InDesign 6.0</xmp:CreatorTool>
		String events of saving history	108C2 or 115F7	<stEvt:instanceID>xmp.iid:972E234B5076E011AAFBC6ED1F893037</stEvt:instanceID><stEvt:when>2011-05-04T15:17:21+02:00</stEvt:when>
		Last file path used	119D8 or 11C4d	%%DocumentFiles:C:\Users\<username>\\Pictures\Sizzla-Soul Deep-Front.jpg %%+C:\Users\<username>\\Pictures\Tulips.jpg
	incx	Previous file format used	15BD2	<xmpGImg:format>JPEG</xmpGImg:format>
Indesign template file	indt	File path for any imported images	CF1E0 or D4F03	%%DocumentFiles:C:\Users\<username>\\Pictures\Sizzla-Soul Deep-Front.jpg %%+C:\Users\<username>\Pictures\Tulips.jpg
		Date file was created	D72AB	<xmp:CreateDate>2011-05-04T15:17:21+02:00</xmp:CreateDate>
		Metadata Date	D72F1	<xmp:MetadataDate>2011-05-04T15:17:21+02:00</xmp:MetadataDate>
		String events of saving history	D3DBA to D3F46	<stEvt:instanceID>xmp.iid:972E234B5076E011AAFBC6ED1F893037</stEvt:instanceID> <stEvt:when>2011-05-04T15:17:21+02:00</stEvt:when>
		Name of application that created the file	D400C or D737C	<xmp:CreatorTool>Adobe InDesign 6.0</xmp:CreatorTool>

Table 2: Graphic design file types related metadata

4 Discussion

From the case study the authors managed to establish the location from which scanned documents were saved to. In this location several other documents were also recognized to indicate the names and original identities of documents. For the action of editing the authors established the names file types and file locations of attached documents. These were fingerprint and human face images inserted onto a copy of the original documents. Following editing, saving actions produced artifacts revealing the names of the saved files, their file types and their locations. These saving actions enabled recognition of potential evidence as they contained the actual counterfeit documents. For the printing action results from registry and log files indicated the names of the printers used and the names of the printed documents.

For user-generated file analysis all graphic design application file types analysed have timestamps as part of their metadata. However only a few of them have the user name of the creator of thefile as part of the metadata. Table 3 summarises the user-gernerated file types. "Yes" in this table indicates that the described metadata is present while "No" denotes that the file type does not contain the described metadata. The headings of the columns are brief names of descriptions of the metadata that was previously tabulated in Table 2.

File format extension	Date of creation	Date of modification	Meta data date	Creator user name	Creator tool	Location of imported images	String events
indd	Yes	Yes	Yes	No	Yes	Yes	Yes
indt	Yes	Yes	Yes	No	Yes	Yes	Yes
incx	Yes	Yes	Yes	No	Yes	Yes	Yes
ai	Yes	Yes	Yes	No	Yes	No	No
ait	Yes	Yes	Yes	Yes	Yes	Yes	Yes
psd	Yes	Yes	Yes	No	Yes	No	Yes
eps	Yes	No	No	Yes	Yes	No	No

Table 3: Summary of User generated file analysis

Given that a digital forensic investigation was initiated on a suspected counterfeit document creation crime, and the document was generated using a graphic design application. And using the identified digital forensic artifacts a digital forensic examiner is able to establish the route at which the document was created and to corroborate the gathered evidence. For example the digital forensic examiner is able to discover the human face, fingerprint, and or bar code images used to create the document. Together with the actual counterfeit document these can be presented in the court for prosecution. By presenting proof of the actions taken during document editing the process followed can provide valuable support in the court.

For content identification, the digital forensic examiner can use the recognized file signatures and the corresponding ASCII text representation to determine the file type of the graphic design applications in question. The file signatures can also be used when searching files from a formatted hard drive. Also an in-depth analysis of user-generated files can assist an examiner in knowing which particular metadata to acquire from graphic design file types and at what offset address.

Recalling that computer evidence is defined as any hardware, software or any data that can be used to prove one or more of the "who, what, when, where, why and how" of a security incident. By reviewing all the artifacts gathered the definition of digital evidence can be confirmed. This is so because all the six questions, "who, what, when, where, why and how" of the digital evidence definition are validated from the results acquired. Briefly clarifying the results: the "who" was specified by an artifact with the user name, the "what", specified by identifying the particular files types from the application, the "when", specified with a registry artifact indicating time of incident, the "where" specified with an artifact showing the file location, the "why" specified with a file metadata extraction revealing the file contents and the "how" with an artifact indicating which application was used for document editing. These results are essential for a digital forensic examiner to know where to look for digital forensic information, guided by knowing what information to find at a named particular location. This speeds up the process of an investigation where graphic design applications were used.

5 Conclusion

The approach outlined in this paper is particularly useful for solving those cases in which document editing is largely associated with a particular application. The approach only addresses case studies involving Adobe products but the same can be done for other graphic design applications. However, the approach doesn't tackle issues where the user only edits a hard copy, scans and prints without using any pre-installed application. Recalling the problem that graphic design applications can be used to create counterfeit documents, and that current digital forensic tools examine a system to find digital evidence but they do not examine a system specifically for the creating of counterfeit documents .The techniques discussed can be incorporated in bigger digital forensic tools like FTK and Encase or possibly the design of a crime specific tool similar to a Porn detection stick, (Parabens software Website, 2011) which is a thumb drive device that will scan and detect pornographic content on a computer. Also, future work can be conducted by carrying out this exercise on other graphic design applications like CorelDraw.

6 References

Adobe XMP Website, (2011) http://www.adobe.com/ products/ xmp/index.html (Accessed 11 November 2011)

Altheide, C., Carvey, H. (2011), "Digital Forensics with Open Source tools". Elsevier. MA USA, pp 2.

Carvey, H. (2009), "Windows Forensic Analysis Dvd Toolkit", 2nd Ed, Elsevier, pp 296.

Casey, E. (2000), "Digital evidence and computer crime", London, Academic Press, pp10.

Cohan, E. (2010), "Towards a science of digital forensic investigation", IFIP Advances Digital Forensics VI, China, pp 17-35

Digital Forensic Research Workshop (2001), "A roadmap for Digital Forensic Research", pp 16.

Gartner Research (2011), "Which operating system will be 2011's bestseller", http://www.gartner.com/technology/research.jsp (Accessed 11 August 2011)

Jones, A., Valli, C. (2008), "Building a digital forensic laboratory", Burlington, Elsevier, pp 285.

Kesler, G. (2011), File signatures, http://www.garykessler.net/library/file_sigs.html, (Accessed 10 October 2011).

Mail and Guardian Website (2011), "Terrorists favour 'easy' fake SA passports", Mail and Guardian online, http://mg.co.za/article/2011-06-17-terrorists-favour-easy-fake-sa-passports (Accessed 17 June 2011)

Parabens software Website (2011), www.paraben-sticks.com/porn-detection-stick (Accessed 9 August 2011)

Reddy, M. (2011) Graphic design file format database, http://www.martinreddy.net/gfx/2d-hi.html (Accessed 10 October 2011)

Solomon, M.G., Barett, D., Broom, N. (2005). "Computer Forensics Jumpstart", Sybex, London, pp 51.

U.S National Institute of Justice (2001) "Electronic Crime Scene Investigation Guide: A guide for First Responders", *NIJ Special report, 2nd Ed,* pp 10-47.

Wall Street Journal (2011), Dow Jones, "Adobe 2Q Net Up 54% On Broad Sales Gains..," http://www.wsj.com, (Accessed 21 June 2011)

Zelkowitz, M.V. (2009), "Advances in computers; information security".Academic Press-Elsevier

Scalable Distributed Signature Detection

R. Hegarty, M. Merabti, Q. Shi and R. Askwith

PROTECT Research Centre for Critical Infrastructure Computer Technology and Protection, School of Computing and Mathematical Sciences, Liverpool John Moores University, James Parsons Building, Byrom Street, Liverpool, L3 3AF,U.K.
e-mail: R.C.Hegarty@2006.ljmu.ac.uk, {M.Merabti, Q.Shi, R.J.Askwith}@ljmu.ac.uk

Abstract

Storage as a Service (SaS) platforms provide users with a convenient and cost effective way to store and share data. The scale and distribution of data in SaS is such that existing signature detection techniques are not suited to the task of analysing data in these platforms. To maintain a practical and effective digital forensic capability, a new approach to the detection of target data in such platforms is required. This paper analyses the potential impact of the widespread use of SaS in particular object storage platforms, has on digital forensic investigations and identifies the key challenges to be overcome. The focus of the paper is the development of a model to distribute the signature detection process in a way that minimises the quantity of resources required to carry out signature detection while at the same time maintaining the accuracy of current techniques and achieving signature detection within appropriate temporal boundaries.

Keywords

Signature detection, Digital forensics, Object storage, Cloud computing

1 Introduction

There has been an explosive growth in the quantity of data stored in SaS platforms. Data from both fixed and mobile devices is routinely stored in "the cloud". Along with the vast quantity of data (Osborne & Slay, 2011) another characteristic of SaS is the distribution of data across many different storage devices. Distribution provides resilience and the ability to recover data in the event of a device failure. Unfortunately the existing image, analyse, present (Grobler, Louwrens, & von Solms, 2010) paradigm of digital forensics is not well equipped to process large scale distributed data (F. Anwar & Anwar, 2011). In particular, the automated signature detection process where each file on a storage device has its hash value computed and compared with a local signature library is infeasible in a distributed environment.

From a practical perspective, it is not possible to image the many thousands of devices, which make up a SaS platform. Ethically imaging these devices in a multi-tenancy environment (Naqvi, Dallons, & Ponsard, 2010) would also be questionable (Burd, Jones, & Seazzu, 2011). Another approach to the preservation, analysis and representation of evidence is required. Fortunately, SaS environments routinely generate and check hash values to validate the integrity of the data they store. These hash values can be extracted for use in the signature detection process. However, there are still challenges to be overcome, firstly the processing requirements for analysing potentially billions of files with a signature library containing the signatures of known target files makes analysis using a single machine infeasible. Secondly, as the signature libraries used in digital forensics contain many millions of signatures. Distributing the signatures to multiple analysis nodes will become infeasible as the number of nodes required carry out signature detection within reasonable temporal constraints grows.

To achieve the scalability essential to carrying out signature detection in a large distributed environment. A model is required to reduce the burden of signature distribution while maintaining the accuracy of the search process. This paper proposes a novel model to minimise the amount of data required to carry out signature detection using multiple analysis nodes. The layout of the remainder of this paper is as follows, related work is detailed in section two followed by a description of our model in section three. Section four describes the experiments carried out to validate our model and finally section five concludes with our findings and proposes future work.

2 Related Work

Object storage services such as Amazon's Simple Storage Service (S3) described in (Palankar, Iamnitchi, Ripeanu, & Garfinkel, 2008) provide users with a flexible and efficient mechanism to store and share their data. They are examples of a subset of Infrastructure as a Service (Rimal, Choi, & Lumb, 2009) providing the storage component. These types of service have a low barrier to entry often providing a limited amount of free storage. By virtue of the scalable elastic nature of these platforms (Delic & Walker, 2008) a pay as you use model similar to that of utility companies (Foster, Zhao, Raicu, & Lu, 2008) (Armbrust et al., 2009) is offered. The detection of illicit data stored in these large-scale storage platforms is the target of the forensic analysis techniques proposed in this paper.

Current digital forensics techniques require physical access to the storage device(s) under investigation. This prerequisite exists due to the requirement to preserve evidence by imaging the device and carrying out analysis on the image (Allen, 2005). This type of approach is not feasible when analysing large-scale highly distributed storage platforms. The storage and bandwidth requirements for carrying out such a task are unrealistic and the ethicacy (Reilly, Wren, & Berry, 2010) of imaging a repository storing data belonging to many thousands of concurrent users would be questionable.

Much work has been carried out to leverage the resources of cloud computing against the task of forensic analysis (SL Garfinkel, 2007). To overcome the challenges associated with the increasing complexity of cases and capacity of modern storage device (Roussev & Richard III, 2004). The authors (Richard &

Roussev, 2006) identified the acquisition phase of the forensic analysis process as being untenable and proposed a system where multiple worker nodes carry out analysis of an image that has been read into memory once. To reduce the time required for analysis by concurrently analysing the image rather than using the sequential approach employed by conventional techniques.

Some work focussed on extending the capability of existing digital forensic techniques used to analyse storage devices to distributed storage. The Forweb search technique proposed by (Haggerty, Llewellyn-Jones, & Taylor, 2008) retrieved blocks from image files found on the world wide web using a crawler. The blocks were analysed using the Forsigs (Haggerty & Taylor, 2006) technique to determine whether a files signature matched that of a signature in the signature library. The technique was accurate but only when applied to a narrow selection of file types (typically JPG, PDF ,GIF) and the reliance on a single host limited the scalability of this approach.

Work has also been carried out to detect copyright infringing content in content delivery networks (Hui, Yin, & Lin, 2009), (Yin, Hui, Li, Lin, & Zhu, 2012). This work was also content/format specific. Similarly techniques for the forensic analysis of Eucalyptus where proposed by (F. Anwar & Anwar, 2011) with the goal of detecting evidence of an attack. While this work is related to our own, the scope is very different with a focus on auditing rather than automated signature detection.

Our previous approach reduced the requirement to transfer large amounts of data in the analysis process by analysing domain specific enhancements to the search technique. We posited that a two stage search with reduced length signatures could achieve a reduction in the required data transfer. Further analysis indicates that when using our previous scheme (Hegarty, Merabti, Shi, & Askwith, 2011) scalability could be limited if large numbers of stage two searches are required. This is due to the reliance on a single node to provide the stage two signatures or carry out stage two signature detection.

3 Distributed Signature Detection

Due to the distribution and scale of data found in SaS platforms, a distributed signature detection technique is required. To overcome the limited scalability of existing signature detection techniques that rely on a single host computer, there are some challenges to be overcome. The first of which is how to affectively distribute the signature libraries used in the signature detection process efficiently? To overcome this challenge we propose a scheme to reduce the burden imposed through replicating and distributing the signature library to each of the distributed analysis nodes.

The hash values used as signatures in conventional signature detection techniques have the ability to represent a tremendous number of unique files. With MD5(Rivest, R., 1992) capable of representing 2^{128} unique files. The probability of a hash value collision occurring is practically zero. While this collision resistance is necessary when hash values are used as signatures in a digital forensic investigation. When there is the requirement to distribute many millions of them for use in a distributed signature detection process, the length of such signatures becomes undesirable.

We propose a model in which the hash values used as signatures are partitioned using two separate techniques. Then utilised in a two stage search to identify target files within a distributed storage environment. The model takes into account the number of analysis nodes, number of files undergoing analysis and the number of signatures in the signature library.

The general model we are proposing selects the first n bits of a hash value for stage one signature detection and uses the remainder of the hash value as the stage two signature. The stage one signatures are sorted and distributed to each analysis node and the stage two signatures partitioned with each node receiving an equal number of signatures as illustrated by the example in Figure 1.

	Stage One Signatures	Stage Two Signatures	
Prefix	All Nodes		
0-3	00125	10294856745920101010293949	Node 1
	10203	9002099200BG191010888819EFE	
	30101	FF901803715018843AB18102937	
4-7	69011	82001038011636829746289101	Node 2
	79202	AA918284773912756591028283	
	70202	B91828187291847536901827648	
8-B	97859	01928385729192B7356781900 91	Node 3
	A0191	819118376454678912717171901	
	B9482	2112132784782B918292813AB98	
C-F	E9101	8881209374762923736491109 29	Node 4
	E9991	1238765351988272716199BB1982	
	F0101	EEF772181008281719127912799	
	<-20bits->	<-108bits->	

Figure 1: Signature Distribution

The partitioning of the first stage signatures results in a reduction in the signature length at the cost of accuracy. The collision rate increases due to the capacity of the signature set made up of n length signatures reducing along with l the signature length. We calculate s the number of stage one signatures for various signature lengths using our algorithm shown in Equation 1.

$$s = \left(\frac{x}{\sum_{i=1}^{z} \frac{1}{i}}\right) 2^l$$

x = The number of hash values input

z = The smaller of number of initial hash value and 2^l

l = Signature length in bits

h = Length of original hash value

Equation 1: Number of Stage One Signatures

With the addition of signatures to the set the probability of a signature being unique falls. To calculate s the total number of signatures in the stage one signature set we sum the probability that each of the signatures added to the set is unique. For each stage one signature generated from the signature library x we determine the probability of each signature being unique by dividing 1 over i the probable number of signatures already in the set. We then multiply the total by 2^l the capacity of the signature set.

$$y = \left(\frac{x}{\sum_{i=1}^{z} \frac{1}{i}}\right) 2^{h-l}$$

x = Number of hash values input

z = The smaller of number of initial hash value and 2^{h-l}

l = Signature length in bits

h = Length of original hash value

Equation 2: Number of Stage Two Signatures

Equation 2 calculates y the number of stage two signatures in similar fashion. The capacity of the signature set represented by the final term 2^{h-l} in Equation 2 is calculated by subtracting l the stage one signature length from h the length of the hash value used in the original signature set.

Using the calculated number of stage one signatures it is possible to determine the rate at which matches will occur, in the stage one search due to the use of a reduced signature length. The stage two search is then used to confirm each match. It should be noted that as the model uses the first n bits of the original hash value as the stage one signature no false negatives can occur, only false positives. In Equation 3 we calculate r the probable rate of stage one matches by dividing the number of stage one signatures s by the capacity of the stage one signature set 2^l.

$$r = \frac{s}{2^l}$$

s = Number of stage one signatures

l = Length of stage one signatures

Equation 3: Probable Rate of Stage One Matches

By taking into account the number of stage one and stage two signatures in combination with the probable rate of stage one matches and the number of analysis nodes .We are able to calculate which stage one signature length results in the lowest overall data transfer. If we assume that, each analysis node processes an equal fraction of the files. Our algorithm shown in Equation 4 calculates the total amount of data transferred during signature detection. Using this calculation we can measure the impact adding analysis nodes has on the amount of data required for analysis.

$$d = \left(ls + \left(\frac{(h-l)y}{n} \right) + \left(\left(r\frac{f}{n}(h-l) \right)\left(1 - \frac{1}{n}\right) \right) \right) n$$

l = Length of the stage one signatures

s = The number of stage one signatures

h = Length of original hash value

y = The number of stage two signatures

n = The number of analysis nodes

r = The rate of stage one matches

f = The number of files

Equation 4: Total Data Transfer Required for Analysis

The amount of data required for the first stage search is calculated by multiplying l the signature length by s the number of stage one signatures. As the stage two signature set is evenly distributed across the analysis nodes the amount of data required by each analysis node is approximately equal. The amount of data required for the second stage search at each node is calculated as h the initial hash value length minus l the length of the stage one signatures multiplied by y the number of stage two signatures, divided by n the number of nodes. Combining the quantity of stage one and stage two data required gives the total amount of data required by each node.

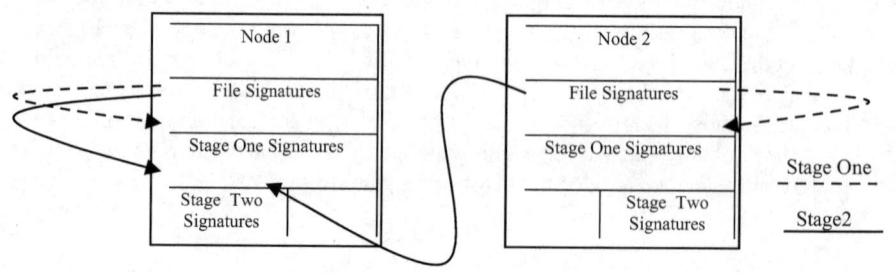

Figure 2: Analysis Node Collaboration

The benefit of the stage two signature set being distributed evenly across the nodes is a reduction in the duplication of data distributed to each of the analysis nodes. The drawback is that further data transfer is required when a stage one match occurs at a node that does not hold the corresponding stage two signatures. This is illustrated by the example in Figure 2 where two nodes carry out analysis, the left hand node does not require collaboration, but the right hand node does resulting in extra data transfer.

To calculate the amount of data transferred between analysis nodes to facilitate stage two signature detection. We calculate the probable number of stage one matches by multiplying r the rate of stage one matches by f/n the number of files at each analysis node. We then factor in the probability that the second stage search must take place at a node other than the node that detected the first stage match. Calculated as $1-1/n$

where n is the number of nodes used in the analysis process. Obviously as the number of nodes increases so does the probability that the signatures required for the second stage node will reside at a different node. The additional data transferred per node is added to the previous total amount of data required per node. The result of which is multiplied by n the number of nodes to calculate d the total amount of data transferred during analysis by all nodes.

4 Experimental Results & Analysis

To validate our model we created a Python script, which conducted two stage signature detection using the optimal signature lengths calculated by our model for various numbers of files, signatures and analysis nodes. We then compared the resulting amount of data required for analysis with that predicted by our model illustrated in light grey on each of the graphs.

The application generated two unique sets of MD5 hash values from random data. The first represented the signature library being used in the analysis process and the second the files undergoing analysis at a single analysis node. Stage one and stage two signature sets where created from the signature library. The stage one signatures where created by selecting the first n bits of each MD5 hash value as indicated by our model. The remaining bits of each hash value were used as stage two signatures. The number of stage two signatures was limited to the fraction of the stage two signature set that each analysis node would contain. The total amount of data required for analysis at each node was calculated by measuring the number of elements in the first and second stage signature sets and multiplying them by their respective signature lengths.

Signature detection was carried out by processing each file signature to produce a stage one signature of the length specified by our model. The stage one file signature was compared with the stage one signature set. If a match occurred the corresponding stage two signature file signature was generated and compared with the stage two signature set.

To account for the additional data transfer required when a second stage file signature needed to be transferred to a different analysis node. Each time a second round search was required an additional $\left(1 - \frac{1}{n}\right) \times (h - l)$ bits where added to the total amount of data required for analysis. The total amount of data required by all analysis nodes was then calculated by multiplying the total amount of data per node by the number of analysis nodes in use.

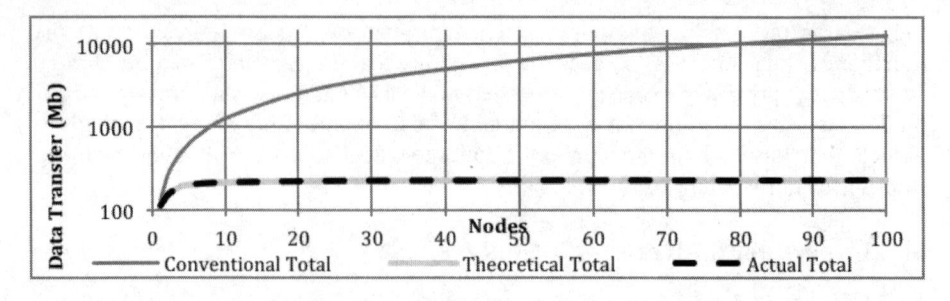

[Figure 3 chart]

Figure 3: Data Transfer Required for Analysis with a 1:1 Signature to File Ratio

In the first experiment we searched 1 million files for 1 million signatures in order to determine how closely our model reflects the actual outcome and identify a trend in the data. Both the first experiment and subsequent experiments were repeated 100 times to enable an average to be calculated. The results are illustrated in Figure 3 note the logarithmic scale. In each experiment the total amount of data required to distributed the entire MD5 signature set to each node was calculated and used as the conventional total for comparison.

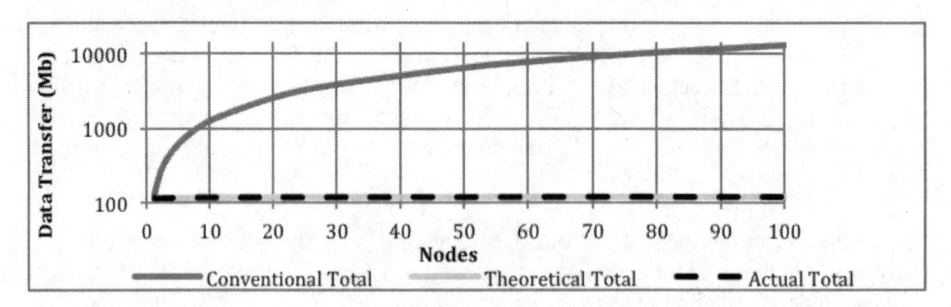

[Figure 4 chart]

Figure 4: Data Transfer Required with a 1:100 File to Signature Ratio

Two further experiments were carried out using different signature to file ratios to illustrate the impact this variation had on the accuracy and scalability of our model. Figure 4 illustrates the total amount of data transferred when 10,000 files were compared with 1 million signatures. The result was a much flatter curve, with the total amount of data required quickly reaching a plateau where the addition of more analysis nodes resulted in a negligible increase in the amount of data required for analysis. The converse was true when the file to signature ratio was increased as illustrated by Figure 5. The curve took much longer to reach a plateau indicating that the addition of analysis nodes drove up the amount of data required more sharply. This was due to the increased number of files being analysed at each node leading to the requirement to use longer stage one signatures, to reduce the false positive rate of the first stage search. Resulting in an increase in the quantity of data transferred to each node. These signatures where duplicated in the distribution process requiring a large amount of data transfer making the curve more pronounced. The curve eventually flattens with the addition of more analysis nodes, reducing the required length of the stage one signatures.

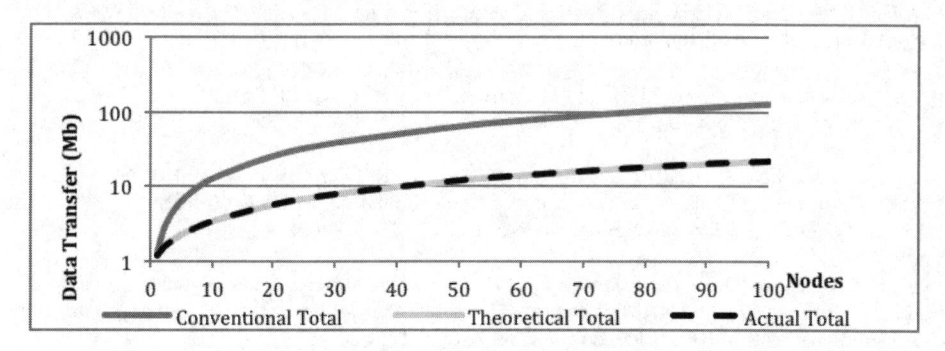

Figure 5: Data Transfer Required with a 100:1 File to Signature Ratio

There is still a considerable reduction in the quantity of data required for analysis in all cases in comparison with the conventional approach. Our experiments were carried out using data that resulted in zero second stage matches; there would be additional data transfer above what the model predicts when matches are present between the file set and signature library. However, the total amount of data transfer would still be lower than if the full MD5 hash values where distributed to each node.

5 Conclusions & Further Work

The data from our experiments indicates that our model can accurately quantify the total amount of data that will be transferred when distributed two stage signature detection is carried out using varying numbers of analysis nodes.

We overcome the limitations of our previous scheme (Hegarty et al., 2011), by removing the reliance on a single node to provide the second stage signatures. As this restricted the scalability of the approach, particularly when large numbers of stage two searches were required. The main contribution this paper makes is a technique that reduces and quantifies the amount of data required for distributed signature detection. This enables informed decisions to be made about the number of analysis nodes to employ in the signature detection process. As the time for data transfer is proportional to the amount of data transferred, our model can quantify the time required for transfer if the availability of bandwidth is known.

Further investigation is required to calculate the time complexity of the two stage search technique utilised in this paper. The focus on data quantity was deliberate as it is likely that the network component of the platform will be the bottleneck in the data intensive task of distributed signature detection.

6 References

Allen, W. H. (2005). Computer forensics. Security & Privacy Magazine, IEEE, 3(4), 59-62. doi:10.1108/09565690610677463

Anwar, F., & Anwar, Z. (2011). Digital Forensics for Eucalyptus. 2011 Frontiers of Information Technology (pp. 110-116). IEEE. doi:10.1109/FIT.2011.28

Armbrust, M., Fox, A., Griffith, R., Joseph, A. D., Katz, R. H., Konwinski, A., Lee, G., et al. (2009). Above the clouds: A berkeley view of cloud computing. EECS Department, University of California, Berkeley, Tech. Rep. UCB/EECS-2009-28. Citeseer.

Burd, S. D., Jones, D. E., & Seazzu, A. F. (2011). Bridging Differences in Digital Forensics for Law Enforcement and National Security. 2011 44th Hawaii International Conference on System Sciences (pp. 1-6). IEEE. doi:10.1109/HICSS.2011.87

Delic, K. a., & Walker, M. A. (2008). Emergence of the Academic Computing Clouds. Ubiquity, 2008(August), 1-1. doi:10.1145/1459229.1414664

Foster, I., Zhao, Y., Raicu, I., & Lu, S. (2008). Cloud Computing and Grid Computing 360-Degree Compared. 2008 Grid Computing Environments Workshop (pp. 1-10). IEEE. doi:10.1109/GCE.2008.4738445

Garfinkel, S.L. (2007). Commodity grid computing with amazon s3 and ec2. Usenix, 7-13.

Grobler, C. P., Louwrens, C. P., & von Solms, S. H. (2010). A Multi-component View of Digital Forensics. 2010 International Conference on Availability, Reliability and Security (pp. 647-652). IEEE. doi:10.1109/ARES.2010.61

Haggerty, J., & Taylor, M. (2006). "FORSIGS: Forensic Signature Analysis of the Hard Drive for Multimedia File Fingerprints." in IFIP International Federation for Information Processing, 232(New Approaches for Security, Privacy and Trust in Complex Environments). Sandton, South Africa. doi:10.1007/978-0-387-72367-9_1

Haggerty, J., Llewellyn-Jones, D., & Taylor, M. (2008). FORWEB: File Fingerprinting for Automated Network Forensics Investigations. Proceedings of the 1st international conference on Forensic applications and techniques in telecommunications, information, and multimedia and workshop (e-Forensics '08) (p. 29). Adelaide, Australia: ICST (Institute for Computer Sciences, Social-Informatics and Telecommunications Engineering).

Hegarty, R., Merabti, M., Shi, Q., & Askwith, R. J. (2011). A Signature Detection Scheme for Distributed Storage. 6th International Annual Workshop on Digital Forensics & Incident Analysis (WDFIA 2011). London.

Hui, W., Yin, H., & Lin, C. (2009). Design and deployment of a digital forensics service platform for online videos. Proceedings of the First ACM workshop on Multimedia in forensics - MiFor '09 (p. 31). New York, New York, USA: ACM Press. doi:10.1145/1631081.1631089

Naqvi, S., Dallons, G., & Ponsard, C. (2010). Applying Digital Forensics in the Future Internet Enterprise Systems - European SME's Perspective. 2010 Fifth IEEE International Workshop on Systematic Approaches to Digital Forensic Engineering (pp. 89-93). IEEE. doi:10.1109/SADFE.2010.28

Osborne, G., & Slay, J. (2011). Digital Forensics Infovis: An Implementation of a Process for Visualisation of Digital Evidence. 2011 Sixth International Conference on Availability, Reliability and Security (pp. 196-201). IEEE. doi:10.1109/ARES.2011.36

Palankar, M. R., Iamnitchi, A., Ripeanu, M., & Garfinkel, S. (2008). Amazon S3 for science grids. Proceedings of the 2008 international workshop on Data-aware distributed computing - DADC '08 (pp. 55-64). New York, New York, USA: ACM Press. doi:10.1145/1383519.1383526

Reilly, D., Wren, C., & Berry, T. (2010). Cloud computing: Forensic challenges for law enforcement. International Conference for Internet Technology and Secured Transactions (ICITST) (pp. 1-7). London, UK.

Richard, G. G., & Roussev, V. (2006). Next-generation digital forensics. Communications of the ACM, 49(2), 76. doi:10.1145/1113034.1113074

Rimal, B. P., Choi, E., & Lumb, I. (2009). A Taxonomy and Survey of Cloud Computing Systems. 2009 Fifth International Joint Conference on INC, IMS and IDC (pp. 44-51). Washington, DC, USA: IEEE. doi:10.1109/NCM.2009.218

Rivest, R., L. (1992). RFC 1321 - The MD5 Message Digest Algorithm.

Roussev, V, & Richard III, G. G. (2004). Breaking the performance wall: The case for distributed digital forensics. Proceedings of the 2004 digital forensics research workshop (DFRWS 2004) (pp. 1-16). DFRWS.

Yin, H., Hui, W., Li, H., Lin, C., & Zhu, W. (2012). A Novel Large-Scale Digital Forensics Service Platform for Internet Videos. IEEE Transactions on Multimedia, 14(1), 178-186. IEEE. doi:10.1109/TMM.2011.2170556

On the Investigation of Application Specific Data within Digital Forensics

H. Baier and A. Brand

Center for Advanced Security Research Darmstadt (CASED),
Hochschule Darmstadt, Darmstadt, Germany
e-mail: harald.baier@cased.de, achim.brand@stud.h-da.de

Abstract

Microsoft Word and Skype are widespread applications in our daily IT life. Up to now, if a computer forensic examination is required, the majority of forensic investigators tends to use commercial software to analyse this application-specific data. However, commercial software is rather expensive and typically closed-source. This paper aims at exploring if an application-specific forensic investigation is feasible by using free available software and whether its findings then still meet the investigators' demands. We contribute to this question by developing a guideline for the forensic investigation of Microsoft Word binary files (aka .doc files) and Skype chat log files. Solely free of charge available tools are proposed for use. In addition, we develop a Python-based, platform independent tool to enable a more in-depth-analysis of .doc-metadata. This tool does not rely on any third-party application libraries (e.g. Microsoft APIs (Application Programming Interfaces)). Furthermore we optimise an existing tool for analysing Skype's .dat files by reverse-engineering the file's structure. Finally, we present a questionnaire completed by 4 experienced practitioners. In spite of the small number of participants their answers underline that our approach meets their needs.

Keywords

Forensic Investigation, Application Forensics, Microsoft Word, Skype, Binary Files, Guideline, Open-Source Software, Anti-Forensics

1. Introduction

Application-specific forensics is a rather new branch in the computer forensic community, but it is very crucial. This is obviously due to the fact that the very basis of all our forensic investigation activities is for the accurate extraction of information from computer-based systems, such that it may be presented as acceptable evidence in a trial (Sammes and Jenkinson, 2007), (Geschonneck, 2011). Therefore, we need to extract all possible information from an application-specific file: the actual content of a file and all its relevant metadata. Thus, we can explore relationships between common actions and associated application metadata (Casey, 2010), (Marshall, 2008). These results can be the cutting edge to solve a forensic case.

Office applications (e.g. Microsoft word), browsers (e.g. Internet Explorer, Firefox), mail clients (e.g. Microsoft Outlook, Thunderbird), or Instant Messaging (e.g. Skype) are of central importance in our daily use of computers. Apart from the standard usage of these applications, some people use them for illegal practices. If this is the case and a trial is supposed to take place, a computer forensic investigator must examine the data which was created by the use of these applications. The majority of forensic practitioners tends to use commercial software which can possibly be rather costly (e.g. standard tools like EnCase, FTK or X-Ways). Additionally commercial software typically is closed-source and hence cannot be inspected (e.g. if we can trust its functionality).

Thus, the question is raised whether it is also possible to conduct such an investigation solely by using free available software and whether its findings then still meet the investigators' demands. As a first contribution we therefore develop a questionnaire, which we sent to established German forensic practitioners (including law enforcement people). Unfortunately only 4 of them answered our questions (though the results are not universally valid, they give us a hint that we are on the right track with our approach). The main statement of their answers is that they have to investigate Microsoft Word and Skype files on a regular basis, they use a variety of rather expensive tools for those purposes, and they are not able to extract all intended information by their current tools.

Additionally this paper contributes to application-specific forensics by developing a guideline for the forensic investigation of Microsoft Word binary files (aka .doc files) and Skype chat log files. Solely free of charge available tools are used in the guideline. In case of Microsoft Word we develop a Python-based, platform independent tool to enable a more in-depth-analysis of .doc-metadata. We call this tool `wordmetadata.py`. Our tool does not rely on any third-party application libraries (e.g. Microsoft APIs). Its source code is open and can thus be trusted. Our tool is superior to previous tools not only due to its simplicity and independence, but also due to its functionality: it is designed to read more metadata from a .doc file than other tools do. We will show that in contrast to current software our tool is able to detect some anti-forensic measures of .doc files.

Finally, reverse engineering of Skype's .dat files is conducted and the file's structure is described. Moreover, the results of our reverse engineering processing are used to improve an existing analysis tool for Skype, the Skype Chatsync Reader. All our tools are available via www.dasec.h-da.de.

The rest of this paper is organised as follows: we first present our questionnaire and the related main results in Section 2. Then we describe our guideline to investigate Microsoft word .doc files and our tool `wordmetadata.py` in Section 3. Next in Section 4 we show how to investigate Skype's .dat files. We close our paper with our conclusions in Section 5.

2. Questionnaire to Forensic Practitioners

In order to learn about the professional investigators' needs for an accurate examination of Microsoft Word and Skype files, we set up a questionnaire, which we sent to experienced forensic practitioners (including law enforcement people) in Germany. They were enquired about their daily work including questions on whether they regularly have to investigate Microsoft Word and Skype files, which tools they usually use for this purpose, which information they are mostly looking for and if they had already had a forensic case where revealed information of these applications helped to solve the case. The answers were given anonymously.

The number of experienced IT forensic practitioners is, however, small. From the 11 contacted persons 4 filled out the questionnaire. Although this is only a small amount of answers, the informative value is nevertheless high due to the huge experience of the investigators in question. In order to stress the qualitative rather than quantitative property of our results, we do not use a percentage presentation of the results.

Some general results of our survey are listed in Table 1. The investigators had to investigate Microsoft Word and Skype files, and in fact, they have to do it on a regular basis. They use a variety of rather expensive tools to fulfil their task. Some forensic cases were mentioned in which information originating from a Word/Skype file helped to solve the case. Finally, as not all relevant information may be extracted, the interviewees appreciate a new application-specific tool.

Do you have to investigate Microsoft Word doc- and Skype-files on a regular basis?	Very often: 1 of 4, Often: 1 of 4, Regularly: 2 of 4
Which tools do you use for such an application-specific forensic investigation?	EnCase, FTK, Ways Application-specific like MS Word, OpenOffice, Skype
Are you able to extract all relevant information using these tools?	Yes: 2 of 4 No: 2 of 4

Table 1: General aspects of our questionnaire

Regarding Microsoft Word some results of our survey are given in Table 2. The relevant information for the forensic investigation is said to be the content, the title, the author, the comments, the last author, the creation date, the modification date, the last print date, the editing time, the used template, the reviewers, and contained VBA (Visual Basic for Applications) macros. Further interesting information includes the name and the model of the printer used, if the file was printed at all.

Some of the survey's interviewees were not able to extract all relevant information using their tools. As a consequence they appreciate a new tool. Missing points compared to existing applications are

- the capability of showing the byte-offset where the inspected information is stored within the doc-file,

- name and model of the utilised printer, and

- the GUID of the computer, where Microsoft Word was used.

Which data structures are of interest when investigating a Microsoft Word doc-file?	Content: 4 of 4 Title: 2 of 4 Author: 4 of 4 Comments: 3 of 4 Last editor: 2 of 4 Creation date: 4 of 4 Last changed: 4 of 4 Last printed: 3 of 4
Are you able to extract all relevant information using your tools?	Yes: 2 of 4 No: 2 of 4
Do you appreciate a new tool for investigating Microsoft Word doc-files, especially if additionally the byte-offset of the inspected data structure within the file is listed?	Yes: 3 of 4 No: 1 of 4

Table 2: Microsoft Word doc-file specific answers of the questionnaire

Finally, Table 3 lists some Skype specific aspects of our survey. The relevant information for the forensic investigation is said to be chat's counterpart, date and time of sent messages, the messages' content, the call's counterpart, the date, time, and duration of a call, the file name of a sent file, the file size of this file, the date and time of the transfer, and its duration. Besides, it is also interesting to learn whether the call was incoming or outgoing. In contrast to Microsoft Word doc-files the majority of the participants were not able to retrieve all relevant information by using their tools (only 1 of 4 was able to do so).

Which data structures are of interest when investigating a Skype file?	Chat communication parties: Chat time stamps: Chat content: Call communication parties: Call time stamps: Call incoming / outgoing: File transfer: Name and size:	4 of 4 4 of 4 4 of 4 4 of 4 4 of 4 4 of 4 4 of 4
Do you investigate only the binary dat-files, the database db-files or both?	Only dat-files: 0 of 4 Only db-files: 0 of 4 Both file types: 4 of 4	
Are you able to extract all relevant information using your tools?	Yes: 1 of 4 No: 3 of 4	

Table 3: Skype specific part of the questionnaire

3. Investigation of Microsoft Word doc-Files

For the investigation of Microsoft Word files it is essential to get, besides the actual content of the file, all the contained metadata, e.g. authors, subject, title, keywords, creation date/time, last saved date/time, last author, last printed date/time, printer name, reviewers and company or organisation name; only to name a few. MS Word stores some of them without any user's influence. In order to be able to conduct a profound forensic investigation of Word doc-files, it is necessary to know which metadata is stored within those files. As a matter of fact, each piece of these metadata could help to solve a forensic case in some way.

When starting our work we were surprised about missing published information on that topic. This paper only addresses Microsoft Word binary files, i.e. .doc-files. According to common market share overviews of Office software (Hümmer, 2011) MS Word has a market share of about 80 to 85% worldwide. Though introduced with Microsoft Office 2003 the XML-based file structure becomes the default format recently. Thus the binary Microsoft Word doc-format is currently the most important office format from a forensic point of view.

The results of our questionnaire of Section 2 show, that most forensic applications do not show all the possible information such as the reviewers, the printer name or the offset to the stored information. Furthermore, the majority of professional tools are closed source and there is no possibility to check if the tool works correctly besides some black box tests. Therefore, we developed a new Python-based open source tool wordmetadata.py to overcome these shortcomings.

In order to understand our tool we first give some short insights to .doc-files in Section 3.1. Then in Section 3.2 we present our guideline to investigate Microsoft Word binary files. For each investigation step we recommend a tool, which may be used free of charge. Finally, we discuss in detail our tool `wordmetadata.py` in Section 3.3.

3.1. Foundations of the Microsoft Word doc-File Structure

Word binary files are using OLE (Object Linking and Embedding) structured storage to manage the structure of the file format (Microsoft Corporation OLE Web Site, 2012). These files are also called *compound files*. The reason for using compound files is that traditional file systems encounter challenges when they attempt to efficiently store multiple kinds of objects in one document. Compound files provide a solution by implementing a simplified file system within a file.

Structured storage defines how to treat a single file as a hierarchical collection of two types of objects, *storage objects* and *stream objects*, which behave as directories and files, respectively. This reduces the overhead and performance penalties associated with storing separate objects in a flat file and also solves performance problems by eliminating the need to entirely rewrite a file when someone changes its content. If there has been a change, new data will be written in the next free space available in the file, and the storage object will update an internal structure which maintains the locations of its storage and stream objects. In addition, structured storage enables end users to treat compound files as if they were a single file rather than several objects. Hence, these files can be copied, backed up, and e-mailed like any other ordinary single file.

A Word binary file uses several structures to organise the file (see e.g. Microsoft OLE 2012). Figure 1 shows the fundamental OLE structures and the byte offsets into the file as absolute offsets from the beginning of the file. The design resembles a classical FAT file system, where the DIFAT (double-indirect file allocation table) is used to find the FAT sectors in the compound files, the FAT is used to find the object chain (like a FAT in the FAT file system), and the mini FAT is used for streams (which are not relevant in our scope). Again like in a FAT file system, directory entries are used to address objects in the doc-file.

3.2. Our Guideline to Investigate Microsoft Word doc-Files

In this section we present our guideline to investigate Microsoft Word doc-files. Our aim is to get hold of the content and the (forensic relevant) metadata of the files, just by using *free available software*, preferably open source software. The reason for this paradigm is reliability and cost-effectiveness of the tools. An additional rich source of open source tools is the web site (Open Source Forensics Web Site, 2012).

Currently we are not aware of any published guideline to investigate Microsoft doc-files and an enumeration of adequate freely available tools. Neither the well-known literature mentioned in this paper nor the up-to-date doc-section of the Forensics Wiki (Garfinkel, 2012) yields support for that. Our aim is to fill this gap.

Figure 2 shows a flow chart on which an investigator can rely on if he has to investigate .doc files. For each step we propose concrete tool(s) to perform this step. The reasoning about our tool choice and a short overview of its capacity is given in the Appendix. However, the overall design of the process model is straightforward.

3.3. Our Tool wordmetadata.py

The answers of forensic practitioners presented in Section 2 reveal shortcomings of currently available software to analyse .doc files. We therefore developed a Python tool named `wordmetadata.py`. It is available via www.dasec.h-da.de. The aim of this tool is to gain as much forensic relevant metadata of a Word .doc file as possible and to be platform independent (i.e. to be usable on any common Operating System). Furthermore, this tool is based only on information provided by the MSDN (Microsoft Developer Network) and therefore it does not rely on any APIs. So, the correctness of the results is transparent and an investigator can rely on the tool.

With respect to the practitioners' needs our tool performs the following tasks on Word .doc files (a sample run of `wordmetadata.py` on a test file `hello.doc` is given in the Appendix):

- Show file system information: file system file size, creation date and time, last modified date and time, and last access date of the file.
- Show internal file size: the file size as given by the internal FAT.
- Show relevant metadata from the "DopBase": creation date and time, last save date and time, revision number, editing time, word count, character count, and paragraph count. This is also the information which is often read by other tools to show the document's metadata.
- Interpret and show all Summary Information Property Set (SIPS) metadata.
- Show byte offset to each value (absolute from the beginning of the file).
- Show number of reviewers and their names.
- Show last save date and time read from the File Information Base (FIB).
- Show printer information where the file was printed.
- Sanity check of file sizes (i.e. comparison of file system based file size to internal FAT stored file size) to recognize anti-forensics.

As the above-noted list and the sample output for `hello.doc` in the Appendix show, some redundancy regarding certain metadata can be noticed, e.g. the creation time is stored in the DopBase and in the SIPS. While analysing the doc-file structure it became apparent that all tested tools read the metadata solely from one source. In contrast, our tool reads metadata from several locations and there is one particular reason for doing so: to recognise anti-foreniscs.

As a matter of fact it could happen that a person tries to obfuscate some chargeable content or action by manually editing the file using a hex editor or an obfuscation tool, e.g. he tries to change the file's creation date and time. Due to the redundancy of this information (DopBase and SIPS), the person probably only changes one location and leaves the further locations unchanged. This obfuscation will be discovered using our `wordmetadata.py` tool. In addition, it might very well happening that he changes the date and time to an invalid value: the value of the seconds for SIPS times must always be ":00" (cf. green rectangle in the output in the Appendix) since Word stores time information in the SIPS only accurate to the minute level. Therefore, the time information in the SIPS plays a vital role and to conform to the specification the `wordmetadata.py` tool calculates these times exact to the second. Thus, if a time stamp within the SIPS contains any other value than ":00" for the seconds, a closer look for a potential anti-forensics manipulation is worth doing.

Showing the offset for each data structure of a doc-file is another advantage of our tool: this feature considerably helps an investigator or any other person comprehending the file structure of .doc files. First, the tool can be used to find the relevant data structure at the corresponding offset. Then, a hex editor/viewer can be used to review and evaluate the findings. Besides proving the correctness of investigation results this proceeding has a positive side-effect on the learning process of forensic relevant data structures. Besides, the findings of the survey in Section 2 demonstrated that three out of four investigators welcome such a feature.

The following example concerning the reviewer's information within a doc-file illustrates how this can be done:

```
sherlock@ubuntu:~$ xxd -s 1938441 -l 40 hello.doc
01d9409: 0700 5500 6e00 6b00 6e00 6f00 7700 6e00   ..U.n.k.n.o.w.n.
01d9419: 0300 6500 7600 6500 0300 6200 6f00 6200   ..e.v.e...b.o.b.
01d9429: ffff 0300 0800 0000                       ........
```

From our sample output in the Appendix we know that the offset to the data structure containing the reviewers is 1,938,441 bytes (see section `Miscellaneous Metadata` of the output). Now `xxd` can be used to seek to this offset and to show the actual value of the data structure. The reviewers are "Unknown", "eve", and "bob". This is correct as Word stores the user "Unknown" as a first reviewer by default into each file as soon as the "Track Changes" feature has been enabled. Thus, the user "Unknown" is no reviewer and therefore there are only two reviewers named "eve" and "bob" (as our tool claims).

A further benefit of using our tool is to perform a sanity check of the file size. When comparing the actual file size (file system file size) to the file size regarding the internal FAT, another way of doing anti-forensics can be identified. Hence, it is possible to append something (e.g. a picture) to an already existing .doc file. A "standard" check using the tools described in this paper would not reveal that there has been another file appended to the .doc file. This fact would not even be discovered by opening the .doc file using Word. As the following listing shows, a file called `picture.jpg` is appended to the test file `hello.doc`. A run of the `wordmetadata.py` on this modified `hello.doc` then reveals after the sanity check that there is an inconsistency corncerning the file.

```
sherlock@ubuntu:~$ cat picture.jpg >> hello.doc
sherlock@ubuntu:~$ python wordmetadata.py hello.doc
------------------------------------------------------
File system information about hello.doc:
------------------------------------------------------
Size:                  3900549 (bytes)
[REMOVED]
File Size regarding FAT:      1972736              (bytes)
################################################################
# Caution: File size sanity check failed.                      #
# Actual file size is larger than file size regarding FAT.     #
# Something could be hidden within the file.                   #
################################################################
```

Furthermore our tool shows information about the printer which was used to print the file, provided that Word (or another Office application) stored this information (typically only older versions of Word behave so). The following listing shows a run of the tool on a file containing some printer information (our sample file `hello.doc` in the Appendix does not contain printer information as declared at the end of the corresponding output). Again we address a dedicated request of the practitioners as discussed in Section 2.

```
sherlock@ubuntu:~$ python wordmetadata.py foo-printed.doc
[REMOVED]
------------------------------------------------------
Printer Information:
Offset to Printer Information:       77812
------------------------------------------------------
Name:           \\srvfps\HP LaserJet 2420 Sekretariat
Port:           Ne05:
Driver:         HP LaserJet 2420 PCL 5e
Product Name:   HP LaserJet 2420 PCL 5e
------------------------------------------------------
End of Printer Information.
```

4. Investigation of Skype Log-Files

Although there are some publications available with respect to Skype network communication (Biondi and Desclaux, 2006), (Baset and Schulzrinne, 2006) for the forensic investigation of Skype log files it is essential to know all used file structures and their content. The latter, however, is not investigated in detail. Information which is of particular interest regarding Skype log files are the following: chat's counterpart, date and time of sent messages, the messages' content, the call's counterpart, the date, time, and duration of a call, the file name of a sent file, the file size of this file, the date and time of the transfer, and its duration. Besides, it is also interesting to learn whether the call was incoming or outgoing. These information is stored in different files, as the following section will describe.

We contribute to a dead-analysis of Skype log files by extending a common existing tool in Section 4.2. Before, we shortly explain in Section 4.1 the locations, where Skype saves forensic relevant persistant data.

4.1. Structure of Skype Log File Folders

The Skype log files are stored in the following folder (henceforth referred to as "log folder") which is dependent on the operating system:

> Windows 7: C:\Users\<osUser>\AppData\Roaming\Skype\<skypeUser>\
> Linux: /home/<osUser>/.Skype/<skypeUser>/

whereby <osUser> is the user name of the operating system user and <skypeUser> is the user name of the Skype user.

As to Windows versions of Skype, all conversations are stored in both, an SQLite3 database "...\main.db" and several binary .dat files within the "...\chatsync" folder. Due to the fact that there is no official documentation for Skype or for the structure of its log files, it remains unclear why Skype stores redundant information using the logs in two different formats.

The Linux versions of Skype, too, stores all conversations in two various ways, in several binary .dat files within the "...\chatsync" folder and in several .dbb files within the log folder ("...\"). However, in contrast to Windows versions there is no "...\main.db".

The main.db is an SQLite3 file, which can be opened with any SQLite3 client to extract the relevant information. Figure 10 (left pane) gives an overview of all tables within the SQLite3 database `main.db`. The most interesting ones are the fields *Messages* (all chat conversations are stored), *CallMembers* (all members of a call), *Calls* (Information about calls), *Contacts* (all Skype contacts), and *Transfers* (all file transfers). Details about an investigation of the `main.db` are given in (Brand, 2011).

For both versions (Windows and Linux) of Skype, there is another interesting file, the "...\config.xml" file, which contains the configuration of Skype and some further information. This file can be opened with any text editor or Internet browser and thus reveals its content. The "config.xml" file contains the configuration of Skype as well as other interesting information. The bulk of the file cannot be interpreted due to the lack of information about the structure. But there are two interesting things stored within this file (see sample `config.xml` in the Appendix): a UNIX timestamp showing the last time when Skype was used by the corresponding user is stored between the start tag "<LastUsed>" and the end tag "</LastUsed>" (which is in this example "20.07.2011 10:32:06 UTC"). In addition, all contacts (Skype user names) of the corresponding user (in this case Sherlock) are stored between the start tag "<u>" and end tag "</u>" (in this example only the Skype user "doktor_watson_001", which means he is Sherlock's only contact).

4.2. Reverse Engineering of Binary .dat File Structure

Due to the necessity of understanding the file structure of the binary .dat files and of providing its description, a programme *Skype Chatsync Reader* (SCR) was selected (Skype Chatsync Reader Web Site 1, 2012), (Skype Chatsync Reader Web Site 2, 2010). The Skype Chatsync Reader parses the log files and extracts the contained conversations. Based on the source code of SCR we were able to do a reverse engineering of the file structure and to describe it. We sketch our results in what follows and point to Application Forensics, 2012, for details.

The "Skype Chatsync Reader" is intended to work with files of Skype version 4.2.0.169. Therefore, this exact version of Skype is needed to perform an initial reverse engineering. As a next step, a test bed with three test users (Sherlock, Watson, and Alice) was created. This test bed contains, in addition to the (up to the present) newest versions for Windows and Linux, also the version of Skype that is supported by SCR. The reverse engineering of SCR's source code combined with a further reverse engineering of the .dat file structure has shown that SCR does not work properly. Therefore, we fixed the bugs in SCR, released an improved version of the SCR, and verification shows that our improved version works now without any failures (for details we refer to Application Forensics, 2011).

The combinations of both reverse engineerings lead into a description of this structure. We released a table providing a complete overview of the identified data structures, which deal with the binary file structure of Skype .dat files. A mapping of this table to a sample hexdump is discussed in Application Forensics, 2011. Our improved SCR is available via www.dasec.h-da.de.

5. Conclusions

We have shown that currently the majority of forensic practitioners tends to use commercial software, but that they are not able to extract all intended information by their current tools. We therefore developed a guideline for the forensic investigation of Microsoft Word binary files (aka .doc files) and Skype chat log files using solely free of charge available tools. In case of Microsoft Word we provide a Python-based, platform independent tool to enable a more in-depth-analysis of .doc-metadata. Our tool is superior to previous tools due to its simplicity, independence, and functionality. Finally, reverse engineering of Skype's .dat files lead to an improved version of the Skype Chatsync Reader. All our tools are available via www.dasec.h-da.de.

6. References

Brand, A (2011), "On the Investigation of Application Specific Data within Digital Forensics", *Master's thesis*, Hochschule Darmstadt, available via www.dasec.h-da.de

Biondi, P. and Desclaux, F (2006), "Silver Needle in the Skype", *BlackHat Europe*

Baset, S.A. and Schulzrinne, H.G. (2006), "An Analysis of the Skype Peer-to-Peer Internet Telephony", *INFOCOM 2006,* 25th IEEE International Conference on Computer Communications, pp1-11

Casey E. (2010), "Handbook of Digital Forensics and Investigation", *Academic Press*

Hümmer T. (2010), "International OpenOffice market shares - Portal – Tutorials, Tipps und Tricks für Webmaster auf Webmasterpro.de", www.webmasterpro.de/portal/news/2010/02/05/international (Accessed 13 February 2012)

Garfinkel, S. (2012), "Forensics Wiki, a Creative Commons-licensed wiki devoted to information about digital forensics", www.forensicswiki.org, (Accessed 28 February 2012)

Geschonneck, A (2011), "Computer-Forensik: Computerstraftaten erkennen, ermitteln, aufklären", *dpunkt-Verlag*

Marshall, A (2008), "Digital Forensics – Digital Evidence in Crime Investigation", *Wiley-Blackwell*

Microsoft Corporation OLE Web Site (2012), "Compound File Binary File Format", msdn.microsoft.com/en-us/library/dd942027%28v=prot.13%29.aspx (Accessed 4 February 2012)

Open Source Forensics Web Site (2012), "Open Source Digital Forensics", www2.opensourceforensics.org/tools/application (Accessed 27 February 2012)

Sammes, T. and Jenkinson, B. (2007), "Forensic Computing – A Practitioner's Guide", *Springer-Verlag*

Skype Chatsync Reader Web Site 1 (2012), "Read Skype Data: Chatsync and SQLite", itsecuritylab.eu/index.php/2010/07/07/read-skype-data-chatsync-and-sqlite/ (Accessed: 21 February 2012)

Skype Chatsync Reader Web Site 2 (2010), "Skype.dat reader is updated", itsecuritylab.eu/index.php/tag/read-skype-chatsync-files/ (Accessed: 21 February 2012)

Appendix

Tools Used in the doc-Analysis-Guideline

Tool	Reason
antiword *(Open Source)*	Antiword is a free software reader for Linux that makes it possible for binary Microsoft Word documents to be read and to be converted into plain text, PostScript, and also into PDF (Portable Document Format) files. Besides, it recognizes pictures within the files and identifies them as "`[pic]`". This also holds for other embedded objects, e.g. an .mp3 or .wav file. Additionally, antiword is ported to several platforms, including Windows and DOS (Disk Operating System). A major asset of antiword is that it can display the content regardless of the used font, font color, effect, style, or any other formatting. This means that content which is not visible by default, such as hidden text or text with white font colour on white background, are being displayed just like everything else.
catdoc *(Open Source)*	Catdoc is quite similar to antiword. Catdoc, too, produces the text of the Word file as plain text. But there is no possibility to export the output to PostScript or PDF and it does not identify contained objects such as pictures or .mp3 files the way antiword does. However, there is an option "`-b`" to process also broken Word files and maybe this helps to read a broken file. Catdoc can be considered to be a second-verification tool in addition to antiword.
Office Visualizer Tool *(Free Available)*	The "Office Visualizer Tool" is a parser for Microsoft Office OLE structured files, i.e. Excel, PowerPoint, and Word binary files. It definitely offers a good possibility to have an organized view of a binary file. The tool is divided into two panes: The left pane (called "Raw File Contents") shows the raw content of the file (in hexadecimal values). The right pane (called "Parsing Results") shows the results from the parsing, i.e. the name of the current data structure, its value, byte offset within the file, size, and type. A click on a certain data structure within the "Parsing Results" indicates the corresponding raw data in the "Raw File Contents" pane and vice versa. This simplifies the discovery of a certain value a lot and helps an investigator to detect the wanted information rather quickly. Due to the high complexity of OLE structured files, the tool cannot interpret every data structure in a sufficient way as an investigator would need it. Thus, this must be done manually, which is far too inconvenient for practical usage in a forensic scope. On the other hand, the tool may just be the perfect choice for some other scenarios, e.g. if an investigator needs an offset to a certain value or if he needs to learn how the OLE file structure works in general.
OfficeMalScanner *(Free Available)*	With regard to an investigation of Word files it can also be interesting to find out which VBA macros are stored within these files. A highly comfortable way to extract the source code of contained macros provides the "OfficeMalScanner" tool for Windows. OfficeMalScanner is a Microsoft Office forensic tool that

	finds malicious shellcode within (legacy binary and new XML) Office files. Additionally, it saves identified VBA macro code to disk. Thus, an investigator can use this tool for both purposes: Checking Office files for malicious shellcode and extracting contained VBA macros without the risk of infecting one's own system, which would happen if the file was opened with Office. Furthermore, it prevents the performing of unwanted calls which could come from the VBA macro. Furthermore, this tool was developed by Frank Boldewin who is well-known in the field of digital forensics.
wordmetadata.py *(Open Source)*	See section "Our Tool wordmetadata.py".
file *(Open Source)*	The Linux/UNIX command "file" is commonly used to determine the file type of a certain file, e.g. if the file is an .mp3, .jpg or .png file. For .doc files it gives a short overview of the file's metadata. This command comes preinstalled with almost any version of Linux/UNIX and so it can be used for a very first inspection of the file's metadata.
extract *(Open Source)*	The "extract" tool was developed to read metadata from certain file types. The website of "extract" says it is able to read metadata from any files, which sounds a bit overbearing. But for the scope of this paper it works pretty well: It gives a short overview of the investigated file's metadata. Additionally, it shows even more information of older versions of .doc files: It is able to extract the revision log of a .doc file, in case there is one. This could be the cutting edge to solve a forensic case. Extract is a good choice if an investigator needs only some basic information about the file's metadata or, for older files, to read the revision log.
Microsoft Word	If the tools mentioned above do not evoke the wanted results, one of the last possibilities is to use Microsoft Word itself to open the document (read-only). The investigator will then see the document from the same point of view as the author or the suspicious person did. However, he has to take into account that he should be well-informed about all the features offered in Word (e.g. hiding pictures and text). Otherwise he might easily be deceived. Additionally, there might also be some VBA macros or other malicious code be contained in the file which could change the file or even infect the investigator's computer. Thus, using Word for the investigation of .doc files should never be an investigator's first choice.

A Sample Output of our doc-Metadata-Tool `wordmetadata.py`

```
sherlock@ubuntu:~$ python wordmetadata.py hello.doc

----------------------------------------------------
File system information about hello.doc:
----------------------------------------------------
Size:                   1972736 (bytes)
Creation Date:          2011-08-13 07:31:18 (UTC)
Last Modified Date:     2011-06-28 14:40:45 (UTC)
```

```
Last Access Date:      2011-08-13 07:31:18 (UTC)
----------------------------------------------------
End of file system information.
----------------------------------------------------
Header Signature:      0xD0CF11E0A1B11AE1    (OLE compound file header)
File Size regarding FAT:    1972736         (bytes)
Offset to 1Table:           1932800
File Identification:        0xA5EC (Word Binary File)
----------------------------------------------------
DopBase Metadata:
----------------------------------------------------
Name:           Creation Date
Value:          2011-06-28 16:21 (UTC)
Offset:         1938923
----------------------------------------------------
Name:           Last Save Date
Value:          2011-06-28 16:40 (UTC)
Offset:         1938927
----------------------------------------------------
Name:           Last Printed Date
Value:          Never
Offset:         1938931
----------------------------------------------------
Name:           Revision Number
Value:          6
Offset:         1938935
----------------------------------------------------
Name:           Editing Time
Value:          0
Offset:         1938937
----------------------------------------------------
Name:           Word Count
Value:          9
Offset:         1938941
----------------------------------------------------
Name:           Character Count
Value:          63
Offset:         1938945
----------------------------------------------------
Name:           Page Count
Value:          1
Offset:         1938949
----------------------------------------------------
Name:           Paragraph Count
Value:          1
Offset:         1938951
----------------------------------------------------
End of DopBase Metadata.
----------------------------------------------------
Summary Information Property Set Metadata:
SIPS Size: 428 (bytes)
Number of Properties:   16
----------------------------------------------------
Name:                       CodePage
Value:                      000004E4
Offset to TPV packet:       1940152
----------------------------------------------------
Name:                       Title
Value:                      Hello World
```

```
Offset to TPV packet:          1940160
-------------------------------------------------
Name:                          Subject
Value:                         Application Layer Forensics
Offset to TPV packet:          1940180
-------------------------------------------------
Name:                          Author
Value:                         sherlock;watson
Offset to TPV packet:          1940216
-------------------------------------------------
Name:                          Keywords
Value:
Offset to TPV packet:          1940240
-------------------------------------------------
Name:                          Comments
Value:                         This files serves as investigation test
file.
Offset to TPV packet:          1940252
-------------------------------------------------
Name:                          Template
Value:                         Normal.dotm
Offset to TPV packet:          1940308
-------------------------------------------------
Name:                          Last Author
Value:                         alice
Offset to TPV packet:          1940328
-------------------------------------------------
Name:                          Revision Number
Value:                         6 (regarding to CodePage)
Offset to TPV packet:          1940344
-------------------------------------------------
Name:                          Application Name
Value:                         Microsoft Office Word
Offset to TPV packet:          1940356
-------------------------------------------------
Name:                          Creation Date
Value:                         2011-06-28 14:21:00 (UTC)
Offset to TPV packet:          1940388
-------------------------------------------------
Name:                          Last Save Date
Value:                         2011-06-28 14:40:00 (UTC)
Offset to TPV packet:          1940400
-------------------------------------------------
Name:                          Page Count
Value:                         1
Offset to TPV packet:          1940412
-------------------------------------------------
Name:                          Word Count
Value:                         9
Offset to TPV packet:          1940420
-------------------------------------------------
Name:                          Character Count
Value:                         63
Offset to TPV packet:          1940428
-------------------------------------------------
Name:                          Document Security
Value:                         0
Offset to TPV packet:          1940436
-------------------------------------------------
End of Summary Information Property Set Metadata.
```

```
------------------------------------------------------
------------------------------------------------------
Miscellaneous Metadata.
------------------------------------------------------
Number of Reviewers:        2
Offset to Reviewers:        1938441
Reviewers:                  eve;bob
Last Save Date (from FIB):  2011-06-28 14:40:45 (UTC)
No Printer Information found.

--- end of script ---
```

A Sample Skype file config.xml

```
<?xml version="1.0"?>
<config version="1.0" serial="18" timestamp="1311157960.8">
  <Lib>
    <Account>
      <LastUsed>1311157926</LastUsed>
    </Account>
    <CentralStorage>
      <SyncSet>
        <u>
          <doktor_watson_001>7bff23a8:2</doktor_watson_001>
        </u>
      </SyncSet>
    </CentralStorage>
</config>
```

A Forensic Text Comparison in SMS Messages: A Likelihood Ratio Approach with Lexical Features

S. Ishihara

The Australian National University, Department of Linguistics, Australia
e-mail: shunichi.ishihara@anu.edu.au

Abstract

Due to its convenience and low cost, short message service (SMS) has been a very popular medium of communication for quite some time. Unfortunately, however, SMS messages are sometimes used for reprehensible purposes, e.g. communication between drug dealers and buyers, or in illicit acts such as extortion, fraud, scams, hoaxes, and false reports of terrorist threats. In this study, we perform a likelihood-ratio-based forensic text comparison of SMS messages focusing on lexical features. The likelihood ratios (LRs) are calculated in Aitken and Lucy's (2004) multivariate kernel density procedure, and are calibrated. The validity of the system is assessed based on the magnitude of the LRs using the log-likelihood-ratio cost (C_{llr}). The strength of the derived LRs is graphically presented in Tippett plots. The results of the current study are compared with those of previous studies.

Keywords

SMS messages, forensic text comparison, likelihood ratio, multivariate kernel density, log-likelihood-ratio cost, calibration

1 Introduction

Due to a continuous increase in the use of mobile phones, the short message service (SMS) is more and more becoming a common medium of communication. Unfortunately, its convenience, low cost and high visual anonymity can be exploited, with SMS messages sometimes used in, for example, communication between drug dealers and buyers, or illicit acts such as, extortion, fraud, scams, hoaxes, false reports of terrorist threats, and many more. SMS messages have been reportedly used as evidence in some legal cases (Cellular-news, 2006; Grant, 2007), and it is not difficult to predict that the use of SMS messages as evidence will increase.

That being said, there is a large amount of research on forensic authorship analysis in other electronically-generated texts, such as emails (De Vel et al., 2001; Iqbal et al., 2008), whereas forensic authorship analysis studies specifically focusing on SMS messages are conspicuously sparse (cf. Ishihara, 2011; Mohan et al., 2010).

The forensic sciences are experiencing a paradigm shift in the evaluation and presentation of evidence (Saks and Koehler, 2005). This paradigm shift has already happened in forensic DNA comparison. Saks and Koehler (2005) fervently suggest that other forensic comparison sciences should follow forensic DNA comparison, which adopts the likelihood-ratio framework for the evaluation of evidence. The use of the likelihood-ratio framework has been advocated in the main textbooks on the evaluation of forensic evidence (e.g. Robertson and Vignaux, 1995) and by forensic statisticians (e.g. Aitken and Stoney, 1991; Aitken and Taroni, 2004).

Thus, emulating forensic DNA comparison, the current study is a forensic comparison of SMS messages using the likelihood-ratio framework. Focusing on the lexical features of SMS messages, we test a forensic text comparison system. The validity of the system is assessed using the log-likelihood-ratio-cost function (C_{llr}) which was originally developed for use in automatic speaker recognition systems (Brümmer and du Preez, 2006), and subsequently adopted in forensic voice comparison (Morrison, 2011). The strength of likelihood ratios (= strength of evidence) obtained from SMS messages is graphically presented using Tippett plots.

2 Forensic Authorship Analysis

2.1 Profiling, Identification and Verification

Forensic authorship analysis can be broadly classified into the subfields of *authorship profiling*, *authorship identification* and *authorship verification*. Commonly-held descriptions of the tasks of these subfields are summarised below:

- *Authorship profiling* summarises the sociolinguistic characteristics, such as gender, age, occupation, educational and cultural background, of the unknown author (offender) of the (illicit) document in question (Stamatatos, 2009).
- The task of (forensic) *authorship identification* is to identify the most likely author (suspect) of a given (incriminating) document from a group of candidate authors (suspects) (Iqbal *et al.*, In Press).
- The task of (forensic) *authorship verification* is to determine or verify if a target author (suspect) did or did not write a specific (incriminating) document (Halteren, 2007).

Using the conventional terminology, the current study is one of forensic authorship *verification*.

2.2 Role of Forensic Expert

Commonly-held views about forensic authorship analysis have been summarised above. However, it is important to explicitly state here that the forensic scientist as a witness is NOT in a position, either legally or logically, to identify, confirm, decide or even verify if two samples (one associated with the offender and the other with a suspect) are from the same person or different people (Robertson and Vignaux, 1995). This is the task of the trier of fact, who can be the judge, the panel of judges, or the jury, depending on the legal system of a country. That is, the ultimate decision as to, for example, whether the author of a document in question is a suspect or not, does not lie with the forensic expert, but with the court. When a forensic scientist presents evidence, it is important that he/she should not violate the province of the trier of fact, and he/she should not even be asked his/her opinion on the likelihood that, for example, it is the suspect who wrote the text in question (Doheny, 1996).

So, what is the role of the forensic scientist? Aitken and Stoney (1991), Aitken and Taroni (2004) and Robertson and Vignaux (1995) state that the role of forensic scientist is to estimate the strength of evidence. That is to say,

> "... the task of forensic scientist is to provide the court with a strength-of-evidence statement in answer to the question: How much more likely are the observed differences/similarities between the known and questioned samples to arise under the hypothesis that they have the same origin than under the hypothesis that they have different origins?" (Morrison, 2009).

The strength of evidence which is the main concern of forensic scientists is technically termed as likelihood ratio (LR).

3 Likelihood-Ratio Approach

The task of the forensic expert is to provide the court with a strength-of-evidence statement by estimating the likelihood ratio. What, then, is the likelihood ratio?

3.1 Likelihood Ratio

The likelihood ratio (LR) is the probability that the evidence would occur if an assertion is true, relative to the probability that the evidence would occur if the assertion is not true (Robertson and Vignaux, 1995). Thus, the LR can be expressed in (5).

$$LR = \frac{p(E|H_p)}{p(E|H_d)} \qquad (5)$$

For forensic authorship analysis, it will be the probability of observing the difference (referred to as the evidence, E) between the group of texts written by the offender and that written by the suspect if they have come from the same author (H_p) (i.e. if the prosecution hypothesis is true) relative to the probability of observing the same evidence (E) if they have been produced by different authors (H_d) (i.e. if the defence hypothesis is true). The relative strength of the given evidence with respect to the competing hypotheses (H_p vs. H_d) is reflected in the magnitude of the LR. The more the LR deviates from unity (LR = 1; logLR = 0), the greater support for either the prosecution hypothesis (LR > 1; logLR > 0) or the defence hypothesis (LR < 1; logLR < 0).

3.2 Related Studies

To the best of our knowledge, Grant (2007) and Ishihara (2011) are the only studies on forensic authorship analysis based on the LR framework: the former is on email and the latter on SMS. The results of the present study will be compared with those of Ishihara (2011) in which the same dataset and evaluation procedures were utilised, but author attribution was modelled by N-grams.

4 Testing

4.1 Scenario

A possible scenario in which SMS messages can be used as evidence of an incriminating act is as follows: the police authority obtained a set of incriminating messages written by a criminal while another set of messages were obtained from a suspect. The relevant parties would like to know whether these two sets of messages were actually written by the same author or different authors. We simulate this scenario in our study. Needless to say, the task of the forensic expert is to provide the court with a strength-of-evidence statement (in other words, LR) so as to assist the trier of fact to make a decision as to whether the suspect is guilty or not.

4.2 Database

In this study, we use the SMS corpus compiled by the National University of Singapore (the NUS SMS corpus) (http://wing.comp.nus.edu.sg:8080/SMSCorpus). A new version of the NUS SMS corpus has been released almost monthly, and we use *version 2011.05.11* which contains 38193 messages from 228 authors. 69% of the total messages were written by native speakers of English; 30% by non-native; 1% unknown. Male authors account for 71%; female for 16%; unknown for 13%. The average length of a message is 13.8 words (sd = 13.5; max = 231; min = 1).

4.3 Selection of Messages

Two message types of author pairs – same-author pairs and different-author pairs – are necessary to assess a forensic text comparison system. The same author pairs are used for so-called *Same Author Comparison* (SA comparison) where two groups of messages produced by the same author are expected to receive the desired LR value given the same-origin, whereas the different author pairs are for *mutatis mutandis*, *Different Author Comparison* (DA comparison). Thus, we need two groups of messages from each of the authors.

This study also investigates how the performance of the system and the strength of evidence (= LR) are influenced by the sample size, i.e. the number of message words used for modelling. It can be safely predicted that the more messages we use, the better the performance will be. However, each SMS message is essentially short, and it is forensically unrealistic to conduct experiments using thousands of messages to model an author's attribution. Thus, as shown in Table 41, we created 4 different datasets (DS) in which the number of words appearing in each message group is different (N = 200, 1000, 2000 and 3000 words). For DS200, each message group contains a total of approximately 200 words. Since we cannot perfectly control the number of words appearing in one message, it needs to be *approximately* 200 words.

DS+N	auths.	SA	DA
DS200	85	85	14280
DS1000	43	43	3612
DS2000	34	34	2244
DS3000	24	24	1104

Table 4: Dataset (DS) configuration: sample size (N) = the number of words included in each message group; auths. = the number of authors appearing in the DS; SA = number of SA comparisons; DA = number of DA comparisons.

In order to compile a message group of about 200 words, we added messages one by one from the chronologically sorted messages to the group until the word number reached more than 200 words. As explained earlier, we need two groups of messages from the same author. For one message group, we started from the top of the chronologically sorted messages while for the other of the same author from the bottom so that the two groups of messages from the same author are non-contemporaneous.

4.4 Features

Following the results of previous authorship studies (De Vel *et al.*, 2001; Iqbal *et al.*, 2010; Zheng *et al.*, 2006), and given the general characteristics of SMS messages (Tagg, 2009), the features listed in Table 52 are used in the current study.

Feature type		Features
vocabulary richness	1.	Yule's K
	2.	Type-token ratio (TTR)
	3.	Honoré's R
lexical: word-based	4.	Average word number per message
	5.	SD of word number
lexical: character based	6.	Average character number per message
	7.	SD of character number
	8.	Upper case ratio
	9.	Digits ratio
	10.	Average character number in a word
	11.	Punctuation character ratio (, . ? ! ; : ' ")
	12.	Special character ratio (< > % | [ ] { } \ / @ # ~ + - * $ ^ & =)

Table 5: List of features.

All features listed in Table 52 are, in a broad sense, lexical features. They can be further sub-classified into the features of *vocabulary richness*, *word-based lexical* and *character-based lexical features*. All feature values are normalised. Features related to sentences and paragraphs are not used in this study as in many cases it is difficult to automatically locate a sentence or a paragraph boundary in SMS messages since the use of upper/lower cases, punctuation, space, etc. does not always conform to standard orthographical rules.

Different combinations of features listed in Table 52 are tested to see what combination yields the best results. However, since testing all possible permutations of these features with various dimensions of a feature vector is time-consuming, we systematically selected only some possible combinations. First of all, we tried all possible combinations of two features $[f_1,f_2]$, and selected the five best performing bi-features. Using these five best performing bi-features as bases, we tested the performance of the tri-features $[f_1,f_2,f_3]$ by adding one of the remaining features one by one to these bases. We repeated this process for feature vectors of higher dimensions.

4.5 Likelihood Ratio Calculation

It is straightforward to combine multiple LRs from different evidence types or features by applying Bayes' Theorem, providing they are not correlated. This is a significant feature of the LR approach as most cases involve many different types of evidence. However, it is obvious that the features listed in Table 52 are correlated in one way or another, thus a simple combination is inappropriate. Aitken and Lucy (2004) addressed the problem of estimating LRs from correlated variables by deriving the multivariate kernel density LR (MVLR) formulae. Following the initial application of the formulae to the data from glass fragments, it has been successfully applied to forensic voice comparison, in particular with acoustic-phonetic features. Please refer to Aitken and Lucy (2004) for the exposition of the MVLR formulae.

A logistic-regression calibration was applied to the derived LRs from the MVLR formulae (Brümmer and du Preez, 2006). Given two sets of LRs derived from the SA and DA comparison pairs and a decision boundary, calibration is a normalisation procedure involving linear monotonic shifting and scaling of the LRs relative to the decision boundary so as to minimise a cost function (see §4.6).

4.6 Evaluation of Performance

Morrison (2011) argues that classification-accuracy/classification-error rates, such as equal error rate, precision and recall, are inappropriate for use within the LR framework because they implicitly refer to posterior probabilities – which is the province of the trier of fact – rather than likelihood ratios – which is the province of forensic scientists – and "they are based on a categorical threshholding, error versus non-error, rather than a gradient strength of evidence ... An appropriate metric ... is the log-likelihood-ratio cost (C_{llr})", which is a gradient metric based on LRs. See (6) for calculating C_{llr} (Brümmer and du Preez, 2006). In (6), N_{Hp} and N_{Hd} are the numbers of SA and of DA comparisons, and LR_i and LR_j are the LRs derived from the SA and DA comparisons, respectively. If the system is producing good quality LRs, all the SA comparisons should produce LRs greater than 1, and the DA comparisons should produce LRs less than 1. In this approach, LRs which support counter-factual hypotheses are given a penalty. The size of this penalty is determined according to how significantly the LRs deviate from the neutral point. That is, an LR supporting a counter-factual hypothesis with greater strength will be penalised more heavily than the ones which have the strength close to the unity, because they are less misleading. The lower the C_{llr} value is, the better the performance is.

$$C_{llr} = \frac{1}{2} \left(\frac{1}{N_{H_p}} \sum_{i\,for\,H_p=true}^{N_{H_p}} \log_2\left(1+\frac{1}{LR_i}\right) + \frac{1}{N_{H_d}} \sum_{j\,for\,H_d=true}^{N_{H_d}} \log_2\left(1+LR_j\right) \right) \quad (6)$$

C_{llr} can be split into a discrimination loss (C_{llr_min}) – which is the value achievable after the application of a calibration procedure (see §4.5) – and a calibration loss (C_{llr_cal}) ($C_{llr} = C_{llr\_min} + C_{llr\_cal}$). Thus, the C_{llr} can provide an overall evaluation of a system while the C_{llr_min} and C_{llr_cal} can specifically show how the discrimination loss and the calibration loss contributed to the overall performance of the system. The FoCal toolkit (http://www.dsp.sun.ac.za/~nbrummer/focal/) is used to calculate C_{llr} in this study. Since C_{llr_min} is the theoretically best C_{llr} value of an optimally calibrated system, the performance of the system was assessed based on the C_{llr_min} values.

C_{llr} provides a scale value which shows the overall performance of a system. A Tippett plot is a graphical presentation which provides more detailed information about the derived LRs. A more detailed explanation of Tippett plots is given in §5.

5 Results and Discussions

The test results given in Table 63 show that it is not necessary to have all features included to obtain the best result. All of the DSs achieved the best result with as few as four or five features (out of 12). The features of vocabulary richness, in particular 'Yule's K' (1) and 'TTR' (2), are good features to be included regardless of the sample size. Other robust features are 'digit ratio' (8), 'average character number' (10) and 'punctuation ratio' (11).

DS+N	features	C_{llr}	C_{llr_min}	C_{llr_cal}
DS200	1,2,10,11	0.94	**0.85**	0.08
DS1000	2,8,10,11	0.72	**0.61**	0.10
DS2000	2,10,11,12	1.36	**0.54**	0.81
DS3000	1,2,4,8,11	1.29	**0.46**	0.83

Table 6: Performance evaluation. DS = Dataset; sample size (N) = the number of words included in each message group; features = best performing feature sets.

It is not surprising, as shown in the C_{llr_min} values of Table 63, that the performance of the system improves as a function of the sample number. DS3000 performs best with a C_{llr_min} value of 0.46.

The results of the current study outperform those of Ishihara (2011) in which datasets identical to those in the current study were assessed in terms of the LRs based on N-gram modelling (the C_{llr_min} values of DS200, DS1000, DS2000 and DS3000 are 0.96, 0.84, 0.72, and 0.62, respectively).

The LRs (uncalibrated and calibrated) of the best performing features are graphically presented as Tippett plots inFigure 1, in which the LRs, which are equal to or greater than the value indicated on the x-axis, are cumulatively plotted separately for the SA and DA comparisons. In Figure 1, a logarithmic (base 10) scale is used, in which case the neutral value is 0. Tippett plots show how strongly the derived LRs not only support the correct hypothesis but also misleadingly support the contrary-to-fact hypothesis.

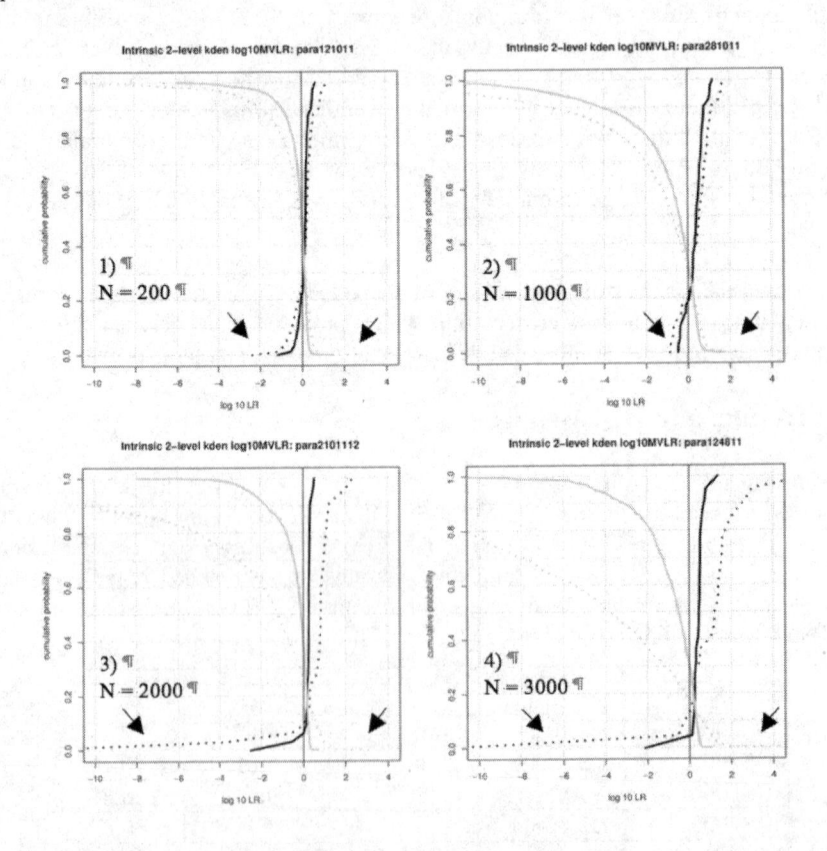

Figure 1: Tippett plots showing uncalibrated (dotted curves) and calibrated (solid curves) LRs for the sample size of 200 (panel 1); 1000 (2); 2000 (3) and 3000 (4). Black = SA comparisons; grey = DA comparison.

The C_{llr_cal} values of Table 63 indicate that DS200 (0.08) and DS1000 (0.10) are better calibrated than DS2000 (0.81) and DS3000 (0.83). This point is clear from Figure 1 (refer to the arrows) in that the uncalibrated LRs which incorrectly support the contrary-to-fact hypothesis are greater in values for the latter than for the former. The application of a calibration favourably results in a reduction in the magnitude of these misleading LRs. It also makes the magnitude of the correct LRs more conservative.

Only for reference, the equal error rates of the four best-performing systems are c.a. 34% (DS200), 24% (DS1000), 17% (DS2000) and 15% (DS3000), which are not bad. Overall, however, the LRs obtained are fairly weak. Using the verbal equivalents of LRs proposed by Champod and Evett (2000), regardless of the sample size, almost all of the calibrated LRs derived for the SA comparisons are between 1 and -1 in their strength, providing, correct or not, only limited support for either hypothesis (in other words, not very useful as evidence). Even for the best-performing result (DS3000), as many as 65% of the calibrated LRs of the DA comparisons are between -1 and 1, again providing only limited support.

6 Conclusions

We performed a likelihood-ratio-based forensic text comparison of SMS messages focusing on lexical features. The LRs were calculated in the multivariate kernel density LR formulae, and calibrated. The validity of the system was assessed based on the magnitude of the LRs using the log-likelihood-ratio-cost (C_{llr}). We demonstrated that the system with lexical features performed better than the one with N-grams. However, we pointed out that many of the derived LRs (calibrated) are weak in their strength as evidence, providing only limited support for either hypothesis.

7 Acknowledgements

This study was financially supported by the ANU Research School of Asia and the Pacific. The author thanks anonymous reviewers for their valuable comments.

8 References

Aitken, C.G.G. and Lucy, D. (2004), "Evaluation of trace evidence in the form of multivariate data", *Journal of the Royal Statistical Society Series C-Applied Statistics*, Vol. 53, pp109-122.

Aitken, C.G.G. and Stoney, D.A. (1991), *The Use of Statistics in Forensic Science*, Ellis Horwood, New York; London, ISBN: 0139337482

Aitken, C.G.G. and Taroni, F. (2004), *Statistics and the Evaluation of Evidence for Forensic Scientists*, Wiley, Chichester, ISBN: 0470843675.

Brümmer, N. and du Preez, J. (2006), "Application-independent evaluation of speaker detection", *Computer Speech and Language*, Vol. 20, No. 2-3, pp230-275.

Cellular-news (2006), "SMS as a tool in murder investigations", *Cellular-news*, http://www.cellular-news.com/story/18775.php, (Accessed 12 January 2012).

Champod, C. and Evett, I.W. (2000), "Commentary on A. P. A. Broeders (1999) 'Some observations on the use of probability scales in forensic identification', Forensic Linguistics 6(2): 228-41", *International Journal of Speech Language and the Law*, Vol. 7, No. 2, pp238-243.

De Vel, O., Anderson, A., Corney, M. and Mohay, G. (2001), "Mining e-mail content for author identification forensics", *ACM Sigmod Record*, Vol. 30, No. 4, pp55-64.

Doheny (1996), *R v Doheny. Court of Appeal Criminal Division. No. 95/5297/Y2*.

Grant, T. (2007), "Quantifying evidence in forensic authorship analysis", *International Journal of Speech Language and the Law*, Vol. 14, No. 1, pp1-25.

Halteren, H.V. (2007), "Author verification by linguistic profiling: An exploration of the parameter space", *Proceedings of the ACM Transactions on Speech and Language (TSLP)*, Vol. 4, No. 1, pp1-17.

Iqbal, F., Binsalleeh, H., Fung, B. and Debbabi, M. (2010), "Mining writeprints from anonymous e-mails for forensic investigation", *Digital Investigation*, Vol. 7, No. 1, pp56-64.

Iqbal, F., Binsalleeh, H., Fung, B.C.M. and Debbabi, M. (In Press), "A unified data mining solution for authorship analysis in anonymous textual communications", *Information Sciences*.

Iqbal, F., Hadjidj, R., Fung, B. and Debbabi, M. (2008), "A novel approach of mining write-prints for authorship attribution in e-mail forensics", *Digital Investigation*, Vol. 5, No. Supplement, ppS42-S51.

Ishihara, S. (2011), "A forensic authorship classification in SMS messages: A likelihood ratio based approach using N-gram", *Proceedings of the Australasian Language Technology Workshop 2011*, pp47-56.

Mohan, A., Baggili, I.M. and Rogers, M.K. (2010), *Authorship attribution of SMS messages using an N-grams approach*, CERIAS Tech Report 2010-11, Center for Education and Research Information Assurance and Security Purdue University, USA.

Morrison, G.S. (2009), "Forensic voice comparison and the paradigm shift", *Science & Justice*, Vol. 49, No. 4, pp298-308.

Morrison, G.S. (2011), "Measuring the validity and reliability of forensic likelihood-ratio systems", *Science & Justice*, Vol. 51, No. 3, pp91-98.

Robertson, B. and Vignaux, G.A. (1995), *Interpreting Evidence: Evaluating Forensic Science in the Courtroom*, Wiley, Chichester, ISBN: 0471960268.

Saks, M.J. and Koehler, J.J. (2005), "The coming paradigm shift in forensic identification science", *Science*, Vol. 309, No. 5736, pp892-895.

Stamatatos, E. (2009), "A survey of modern authorship attribution methods", *Journal of the American Society for Information Science and Technology*, Vol. 60, No. 3, pp538-556.

Tagg, C. (2009), *A Corpus Linguistics Study of SMS Text Messaging*, PhD thesis, The University of Birmingham.

Zheng, R., Li, J.X., Chen, H.C. and Huang, Z. (2006), "A framework for authorship identification of online messages: Writing-style features and classification techniques", *Journal of the American Society for Information Science and Technology*, Vol. 57, No. 3, pp378-393.

Forensic Analysis of User Interaction with Social Media: A Methodology

J. Haggerty[1], M.C. Casson[2], S. Haggerty[3] and M.J. Taylor[4]

[1]School of Computing, Science & Engineering, University of Salford, Greater Manchester, M5 4WT
[2]Henley Business School, University of Reading, Reading, RG6 6UD
[3]School of Humanities, University of Nottingham, Nottingham, NG7 2RD
[4]School of Computing & Mathematical Sciences, Liverpool John Moores University, Liverpool, L3 3AF
e-mail : J.Haggerty@salford.ac.uk; m.c.casson@reading.ac.uk; sheryllynne.haggerty@nottingham.ac.uk; M.J.Taylor@ljmu.ac.uk

Abstract

The increasing use of social media, whereby users interact online, ensures that it will provide a useful source of evidence for the forensics examiner. Due to the dynamic nature of this environment, current approaches for its analysis are not without their limitations. This paper posits a novel inter-disciplinary methodology for the forensic analysis of user interaction with social media. In particular, it presents an approach for the quantitative analysis of user engagement to identify relational and temporal dimensions of evidence that will be relevant to an investigation. In this way, it may be used to support the identification of individuals who might be 'instigators' in a criminal event orchestrated via social media, or a means of potentially identifying those who might be involved in the 'peaks' of activity. In order to demonstrate the applicability of this methodology, this paper applies it to a case study of users posting to a social media Web site.

Keywords

Digital forensics, social media, social network analysis, regression analysis

1 Introduction

Social media, whereby users interact online, plays an increasingly important role in our lives due to accessibility from heterogeneous computing devices. Sites that are widely used range from those where users can post comments in near-real time to social networking services. For example, Twitter, the micro-blogging site, has 100 million users with over 230 million 'tweets' sent each day (Business Insider, 2011). Facebook has 800 million users, of which more than 350 million access the service through mobile devices (Facebook, 2012). Interaction with social media will therefore provide a useful source of digital evidence during an investigation. For example, a number of people used social media to encourage rioting, criminal damage and theft during civil unrest in the UK during August 2011 and have since been sentenced to significant terms in prison (see for example BBC, 2011). Current forensics tools find this environment problematic as they focus on the extraction of evidence from storage media.

This paper posits a novel inter-disciplinary approach for the forensic analysis of social media. In particular, it presents a methodology for the quantitative examination of social media users pertinent to a forensics investigation through temporal social network and regression analysis. In this way, it may be used to support the identification of individuals who might be 'instigators' in a criminal event orchestrated via social media, or a means of potentially identifying those who might be involved in the 'peaks' of activity. Unlike previous approaches to social network analysis in digital forensics whereby the relationships *between* actors are identified and analysed, this approach focuses on the relationship *with* the social media service itself to identify those actors of significance over time. Therefore, the proposed methodology enhances a forensics investigation by analysing the relational *and* temporal dimensions of actors' interactions with social media. Moreover, it identifies those actors that have a statistically significant relationship with the social media under investigation to triage evidence.

This paper is organised as follows. Section 2 discusses related work. Section 3 posits the methodology and describes two models for the analysis of social media. Section 4 presents the results of applying the methodology to a case study. Finally, we make our conclusions in section 5 and discuss further work.

2 Related work

Social network analysis has been proposed as an aid for digital investigations, especially in those that involve the interaction of actors online. For example, Haggerty *et al* (2011) use the Enron email corpus as a case study to propose a method for the triage and analysis of email data. Dellutri *et al* (2009) focus on the identification of social networks to reconstruct a user's profile by combining a smartphone's data with social relationships found on the Internet. However, these approaches have in common that they focus on the details of extracting and identifying evidence.

Current tools for social network analysis that may be used for digital forensics investigations involving social media often provide static visualisations. Applications such as *Pajek* (Vlado, 2012) visualise network information via the connection of vertices through arcs and edges. In addition, weighting may be applied to network edges to represent strength of ties (Perer and Schneiderman, 2009). The common issue with these static social network visualisations is that they do not represent temporal changes in the network, including an individual actor's engagement over time. Thus, Falkowski *et al* (2006) suggest an approach for analysis of subgroup evolution in social networks. This approach uses a number of views to facilitate analysis and displays the network in a graph, such as those used in static approaches, but laid out along a temporal plain. Hu and Gong (2010) present a visualisation of individuals' spatial-temporal social networks through three-dimensional graphs. Belingerio *et al* (2010) use three-dimensional graphs combined with hierarchical trees to identify eras in social networks. These approaches have in common that they centre on relationships between actors, i.e. they assume direct communications between them. However, in many social media environments data is posted on the site for all to see, rather than direct communication. Therefore, the relationship is often one of actor-to-Web-site rather than actor-to-actor. Thus, other approaches must be used for forensic analysis of social media.

Recent work has identified regression analysis as an approach to investigate user interaction with social media. For example, Shwu-Min Horng (2010) uses multiple regressions for the analysis of connections between users' behaviour on social network sites and data collected from Google Analytics. Kumar and Saha (2009) use regression analysis with other techniques for the data mining of Web blog entries to detect user sentiments. Beck (2011) uses logistic regression analysis to detect spam and phishing attacks over the Twitter network. However, these approaches have in common that they are not focused on the requirements of a forensics investigation. This paper therefore posits a methodology to incorporate regression analysis into a forensics investigation of social media.

3 Forensic analysis of user interaction with social media

Social networks formed through social media are dynamic, evolve over time and react to endogenous and exogenous events suggesting relational *and* temporal dimensions of this type of media. They therefore not only provide evidence of user engagement but also an indication of how the network has developed over time. Of interest to the forensics examiner investigating social media would be the following:

- Who are the key actors identified through the social media?
- What is an actor's relationship with the social media under investigation?
- What statements can be asserted about an actor's social media usage?
- Are there key periods of activity and relationships providing evidence?
- Are there specific actors that drive the narrative on the social media?
- Is there a pattern of interaction that may be identified?
- Network reactions to endogenous and/or exogenous events?

It should be noted that actors who post on social media have varying levels of relationship with the other actors in the network(s) observed. In some cases, the actors will form personal relationships, whereas in others, they do not. What they do have in common is that they have a relationship *with* the social media itself. Therefore, current tools and techniques used in the analysis of social networks, for example in email communications, do not fully meet the requirements for the analysis of social media. Moreover, data is made publicly available by the actors actively engaging with the social media. This is contrast to social networks formed through other communications media, such as email, whereby forensic analysts must adhere to relevant laws to protect privacy.

As discussed in the previous section, the common issue with static social network visualisations is that obviously they do not represent temporal changes in the network. They are therefore limited in answering the questions above if used in isolation. Temporal social network analysis aims to answer the needs of forensics examiners by analysing change over time by highlighting 'real' relationships; actors in contact *at* a particular point in time and shown *over* a period of time. It aims to provide an interactive visualisation of time-varying (social) network data for examiners to interact with. This interaction can provide new questions for the examiner. Importantly, it identifies macro trends in networks to meet the shortcomings of static social network analysis tools.

Two models are posited which examine different aspects of network behaviour and identify statistically significant actors. Model 1 identifies the actors who most regularly interact with the social media and the periods that experience the most user interaction. This has the advantage that the results provide information that can be used to test whether the variations between periods of time and between actors are statistically significant or not, i.e. to determine whether it is likely that they were produced purely by random fluctuations or whether systematic factors, such as endogenous and exogenous events relevant to the investigation, are at work. This is achieved through a panel regression. Panel data analysis is an increasingly popular form of longitudinal data analysis among social science researchers. A panel is a cross-section or group of individuals who are surveyed periodically over a given time span.

Model 1 assumes that there are N individuals indexed $i = 1,..., N$ and T times indexed $t = 1,..., T$. A matrix Y (known as the interaction matrix) is created with N columns and T rows, and therefore with NT cells. The entries in the cells are binary: one if a particular individual interacts in a particular period and zero otherwise. All actors who belong to the network at any time should normally be included. A panel regression model is specified in which the probability that individual i interacts in period t is

$$\text{Prob}(y_{it} = 1) = c + a_t + b_i + u_{it} \tag{1}$$

where y_{it} is the binary element in the ith column and tth row, c is a constant, measuring the relative frequency with which an actor on average interacts with the social media, a_t is a period-specific factor reflecting the above-average popularity of the site at time t, and b_i is an actor-specific factor reflecting the disposition of the ith actor to interact more frequently than average. The variable u_{it} represents an unobservable random disturbance which can be either positive or negative; it is assumed to have zero mean and a constant variance, independent of i and t.

Model 2 identifies particular time patterns in interaction. It tests for the existence of a deterministic linear time trend by which interaction either increases or decreases over time at a constant absolute rate. It also tests for persistence in interaction patterns, whereby interaction at the immediately previous period increases the probability of interaction in the current period. It also tests for delayed persistence, whereby interaction in the last-but-one period increases the probability of interaction in the current period. Testing for persistence also provides a test for alternation, whereby interaction in the previous period (or the period before that) discourages interaction in the current period and non-interaction in the previous period (or the period before that) increases it.

A disadvantage of model 1 is that although it contains a large number of time dummies, it does not directly address the question of whether there are systematic time patterns in interaction. This can be remedied by replacing the time dummies with more meaningful variables. These include a linear time trend, t, whose values range from 0 (at the start of the period) to $T-1$ at the end, as well as lagged values of the dependent variable.

$$\text{Prob}(y_{it} = 1) = c + a_0 t + a_1 y_{it-1} + a_2 y_{it-2} + b_i + u_{it} \qquad (2)$$

A time trend variable, t, is formed by stacking N sequences on top of each other. A variable y_{-1}, representing a single lag in the dependent variable is generated by taking the values of the dependent variable for each individual for periods from 0 to $T-1$, adding an empty cell at the beginning, and then stacking them as before. A double lag variable, y_{-2}, is captured by taking the values of the dependent variable for each individual for periods 0 to $T-2$, adding two empty cells at the beginning, and then stacking them in the same way. The estimated regression is

$$y = c + \sum_t a_t w_t + a_0 t + a_1 y_{-1} + a_2 y_{-2} + \sum_i b_i x_i \qquad (3.1)$$

where for some $i = j$,

$$b_j = 0; \qquad (3.2)$$

The parameters a_0, a_1, a_2, b_i are estimators of the parameters of the model represented by equation (2).

The social media interpretation of the results obtained from employing these models to actors engaging *with*, rather than passively *following*, social media is as follows. Positive results identify actors that engage with the network during key periods and when the network is more active. This could occur for a number of reasons, including: actors interact with the social media because something is affecting the network requiring the whole community to react; actors joining in an upswell of popularity of the social media; are online community leaders whose virtual presence is required. Positive results suggest that these actors are independent of the network but will interact when it is in their interest to do so. Negative results identify actors who engage with the network when interaction is less popular or re-engage even when interaction is low. This could be for a number of reasons, including: actors new to this particular social media and wish to engage with others in the online community; interact with the network in a decline from a popular period (actors who heard the social media was active but interact as engagement decreases); actors who require the status that the social media interaction provides; leading actors of the network itself. Negative results suggest that these actors are more dependent on the network and so make every effort to interact.

4 Case study and results

To demonstrate the applicability of the proposed methodology, this section presents a case study of users posting comments on a social media Web site. Depending on the investigation, the time periods will be hours for fast-moving events, such as riots, or days for longer-term interactions, such as suspects involved in the dissemination of indecent images of children. For ease of reference, we assume hours in this case study. As the aim of this paper is to posit the quantitative methodology, qualitative analysis is not discussed. However, it is recognised that qualitative analysis, such as reading the posts made by users, would be an important element of the overall investigation.

Figure 1 applies the network data to a temporal social network analysis tool, *Matrixify* (Haggerty and Haggerty, 2011). This tool visualises the network data as a two-dimensional matrix to show individual user interaction with the network over time. It also provides a number of menus to provide alternative views and analysis of the network, such as graph layouts, network statistics and qualitative analysis tools. The aim of using temporal analysis is to visually explore the data in order to provide a more nuanced and sophisticated overview of the network, assess actor interaction and identify change over time. It does not aim to *answer* questions; but to *raise* questions around the data not evident in other forms. These questions can then, for example, guide the forensic examiner to relevant sources of further analysis or challenge existing hypotheses and theories.

Time periods are placed on the X axis and actors that engaged with the network during this time are represented on the Y axis by name. Their involvement and role in the network is indicated by coloured dots. Thus, individual engagement with the network is represented horizontally and user engagement on a period-by-period basis is viewed vertically. Ten-hour markers are included to aid reference. In addition, the analyst can specify colours within the tool. In this case, normal users are coloured blue, whilst those users with a higher level of access, for example, moderators or administrators are coloured red. This aids analysis of actor engagement by role.

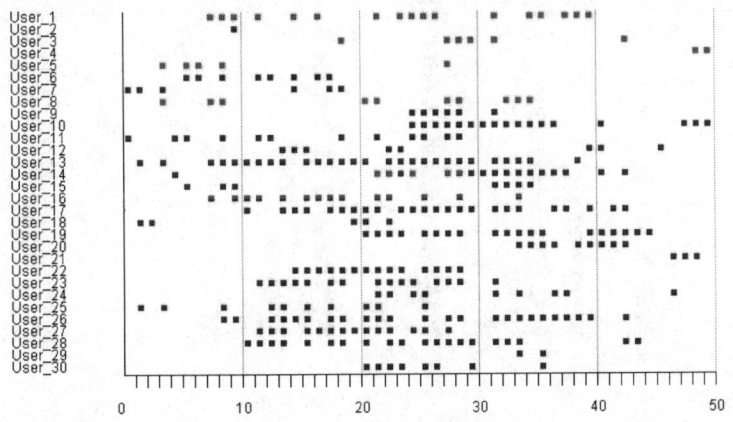

Figure 1: Temporal view of user interaction over time

Figure 1 highlights the trends in interaction whereby engagement is low initially, it then sees a period of higher interaction between 15-35 hours, before engagement decreases. In addition, it raises a number of questions about network engagement that may be useful during an investigation. First, why are some actors active for only a short time and others active for longer? Do some not find the social media useful, and if so, why? Do they interact elsewhere? Conversely, do the long-term actors dominate the network, and do they constitute an online clique? Second, why is the network denser in particular periods (in this case, the 10s, 20s and 30s)? Why does this change significantly in the mid-30s? Are exogenous or endogenous events driving this? Third, what are the causes for the relative lack of actor involvement in certain periods? In the case study this occurs in the 0s and 40s. Why are these periods particularly lacking in long-term actor involvement? Are actors interacting with other social media? Fourth, how does shifting actor engagement impact on access to information or the reaction to exogenous events, particularly those relevant to the forensics investigation? Fifth, is there a long-term survival of the network(s) or has it a natural life-cycle?

Of interest in the results for statistically significant actors and for network analysis is whether an actor has a positive or negative relationship with the social media. Therefore, models 1 and 2 are applied to the social media engagement data. As discussed in the previous section, a positive result indicates statistically significant actors who interact with the social media during key periods and when it is increasingly or decreasingly active. A negative result indicates those actors who engage with the social media even when user engagement is low. This overview by 10-hour periods enables the investigator to assert statistical trends in user interaction and changes in the social media usage. Figure 2 illustrates the total number of actors within a subset and the numbers of positive and negative statistically significant actors.

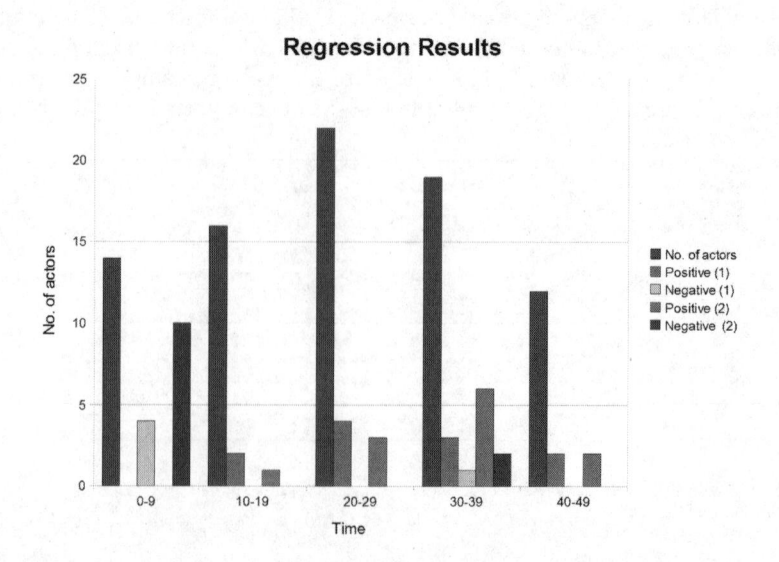

Figure 2: Results of the regression analysis

As figure 2 demonstrates, relationships with the social media change over time, as indeed, do the number of actors involved in engaging with the social media. During 0-9 hours, statistically significant actors have a negative relationship with the social media suggesting a core of actors who interact with the social media even at less popular times. This is reversed in the next two periods, reflecting an upswell of user engagement. This would direct the forensic examiner in their analysis as it indicates a change in user interaction and may provide an indication that endogenous or exogenous network events relevant to the investigation are occurring. Therefore, they will be interested in the qualitative analysis of the posts being made at this time. The period 30-39 indicates another change in relationships with the social media where interaction occurs at both popular and less popular times. Finally, the network declines with users sporadically interacting with the network.

In order to direct (and triage) the qualitative examination, individual actors highlighted by the regression analysis are clustered by period to identify those that are actively reacting to endogenous and exogenous events. Figure 3 illustrates the relational view by 10-hour periods. These actors are clustered by their relationship with the social media, where non-statistically significant actors are on the left, positive actors are top right and negative actors are bottom right. This provides a static network representation and is produced in the *Matrixify* tool. If an actor posts in the same time period as another, a relationship (represented by a line) is formed. This can also be used by the forensics examiner to identify actors that form relationships through the social media, for example, reacting to posts by other actors or to network events (although relational analysis is not the focus of this paper).

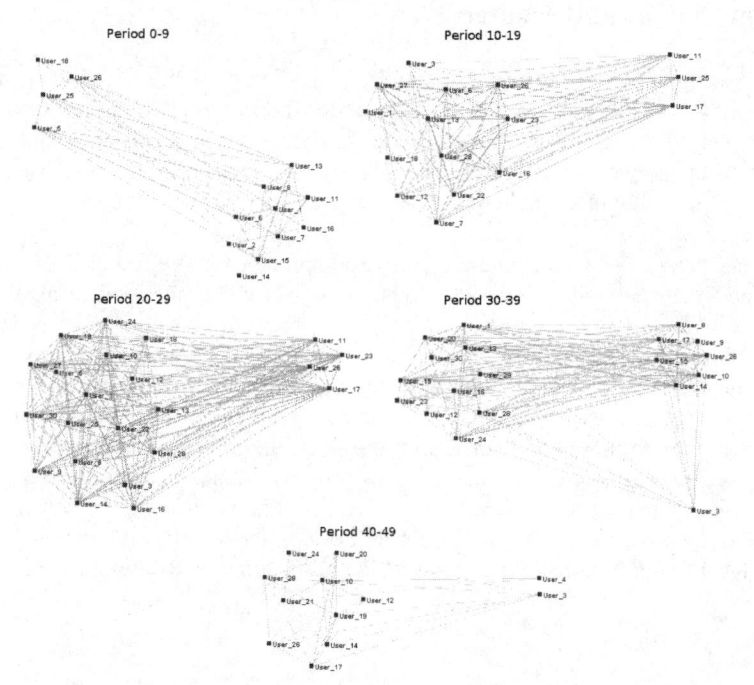

Figure 3: Network cluster analysis identifying key actors

As illustrated in figure 3, the majority of actors who post in the period 0-9 have a negative relationship with the social media. These may be actors who have a long-term relationship with the social media. This changes in the next two periods where actors of note are positive and fewer in numbers. Of interest to the forensic examiner is User_11 who is identified in all three periods. In addition, User-17 is highlighted in periods 10-29. User_26 is highlighted in periods 20-39. Finally, in period 40-49, User_3 and User_4 are highlighted as interaction with the social media decreases. These actors would be of note as they are contributing to the evidentiary evolution of the network, fuelling or reacting to endogenous and exogenous events. This would direct the forensics examiner to potential posts requiring qualitative analysis.

This section has presented a case study to demonstrate the applicability of the proposed methodology for the analysis of relational and temporal dimensions of evidence in social media. The temporal social network analysis highlights macro trends in user interaction and raises further questions regarding user engagement. The regression analysis identifies the nature of actor relationships with the social media over time. Finally, the cluster analysis highlights those individual actors that have a statistically significant relationship with the social media. In this way, the methodology posited in this paper supports the identification of individuals who might be 'instigators' in a criminal event orchestrated via social media, or a means of potentially identifying those who might be involved in the 'peaks' of activity. Moreover, the methodology could be utilised to triage potentially large data sets that the forensics examiner may encounter prior to a qualitative analysis.

5 Conclusions and further work

The increasing use of social media, whereby actors interact with Web sites, ensures that it will provide a useful source of evidence for the forensics examiner. Currently, an examiner will conduct a time-consuming qualitative analysis of social media relevant to their investigation. Current tools, such as those used for social network analysis, do not fully meet the requirements of this type of investigation.

This paper presents a novel inter-disciplinary approach for the forensic analysis of social media. In particular, it posits a methodology for the quantitative analysis of social media users to identify the relational and temporal dimensions of evidence that will be relevant to an investigation. Given the potentially large data sets in this environment, the proposed methodology may also be used to triage data. In order to demonstrate the proposed methodology, this paper has applied it to a case study of users interacting through social media. In this way, the forensics examiner is able to gain a more sophisticated and nuanced view of user interaction and is able to assert those actors that have a statistically significant relationship with the social media under investigation. Future work will further develop the techniques presented in this paper. In particular, it aims to incorporate tools for automated qualitative analysis.

6 References

BBC (2011), http://www.bbc.co.uk/news/uk-england-hereford-worcester-16185152. (Accessed 7 February, 2012)

Beck, T. (2011), "Analyzing Tweets to Identify Malicious Messages", *Proceedings of the IEEE International Conference on Electro/Information Technology*, Minnesota, USA, 2011, pp. 1-5.

Berlingerio, M., Coscia, M., Giannotti, F., Monreale, A. and Pedreschi, D. (2010), "Towards Discovery of Eras in Social Networks", *Proceedings of the M3SN 2010 Workshop, in conjunction with ICDE2010*, California, USA, 2010, pp. 278-281.

Business Insider (2011), http://articles.businessinsider.com/2011-09-13/tech/30148448 _1_dick-costolo-twitter-s-ceo-tweets. (Accessed 7 February, 2012)

Dellutri, F., Laura, L., Ottaviani, V. and Italiano, G.F. (2009), "Extracting Social Networks from Seized Smartphones and Web Data", *Proceedings of the 1st International Workshop on Information Forensics and Security*, London, UK, 2009, pp. 101-105.

Facebook Statistics (2012), http://www.facebook.com/press/info.php?statistics. (Accessed 9 January, 2012)

Falkowski, T., Bartelheimer, J. and Spiliopoulou, M. (2006), "Mining and Visualizing the Evolution of Subgroups in Social Networks", *Proceedings of the International Conference on Web Intelligence*, Hong Kong, 2006, pp. 52-58.

Haggerty, J. and Haggerty, S. (2011), "Temporal Social Network Analysis for Historians: A Case Study", *Proceedings of the International Conference on Visualization Theory and Applications (IVAPP 2011)*, Algarve, Portugal, 2011, pp. 207 - 217.

Haggerty, J., Karran, A.J., Lamb, D.J. and Taylor, M.J. (2011), "A Framework for the Forensic Investigation of Unstructured Email Relationship Data", *International Journal of Digital Crime and Forensics*, Volume 3 Number 3, September 2011, pp. 1-18.

Hu, B. and Gong, J. (2010), "Modeling Individual-Based Social Network with Spatial-Temporal Information", *Proceedings of the International Conference on Management and Service Science*, Wuhan, China, 2010, pp. 1-4.

Kumar Pal, J. and Saha, A. (2010), "Identifying Themes in Social Media and Detecting Sentiments", *Proceedings of the International Conference on Advances in Social Networks Analysis and Mining*, Odense, Denmark, 2010, pp. 452-457.

Perer, A. and Schneiderman, B. (2009), "Integrating Statistics and Visualization for Exploratory Power: From Long-Term Case Studies to Design Guidelines", *IEEE Computer Graphics and Applications,* May/June, 2009, pp. 39-51.

Shwu-Min Horng (2010), "Analysis of Users Behavior on Web 2.0 Social Network Sites: An Empirical Study", *Proceedings of the 7th International Conference on Information Technology: New Generations*, Nevada, USA, 2010, pp. 454-459.

Vlado, A. (2012), http://vlado.fmf.uni-lj.si/pub/networks/pajek/. (Accessed 7 February, 2012)

a
Using Hypothesis Generation in Event Profiling for Digital Forensic Investigations

L. Pan, N. Khan and L. Batten

School of IT, Deakin University, Melbourne, Australia
e-mail: {l.pan; nakh; lmbatten}@deakin.edu.au

Abstract

The traditional manual approach to the investigation of digital data is no longer feasible as the amount of data which can be saved on hard drives grows out of control. In addition, it is usually necessary to consider data across extensive networks of devices in order to obtain a realistic picture of an investigation and ensure that no evidence is overlooked. The need for an automated approach to forensic digital investigation has therefore been recognized for some years, and several authors have developed frameworks in this direction. The aim of this paper is to enhance and move beyond current work by focusing on hypothesis generation in the later part of the analysis phase. In doing so, we present, for the first time in this context, a formal definition of the word 'hypothesis' and also present an extensive case study to illustrate its usefulness and the method of hypothesis generation and analysis. The scientific approach taken here to hypothesis generation directly supports the investigation procedure and also promotes its acceptance by a court of law.

Keywords

Digital forensics, Hypothesis generation, Confidence level.

1 Introduction

Digital forensics is the investigation of an event based on digital information and is often undertaken with the aim of extracting evidence which will be tenable in a court of law (Carrier 2006) and (Willassen 2008). The last decade has seen an influx of research work designed to assist the forensic investigator to move from the historically manual approach towards an automated, and therefore also reproducible, approach to the discovery of digital evidence (Batten and Pan 2011), Marrington et al. 2010), and (Jankun-Kelly et al. 2009). Automated methods rely on a logical and consistent analysis from which conclusions can be drawn. (Carrier 2006) and (Marrington 2009) both developed automated methods of describing a computer system and its activity over a fixed period of time; the former focused on the raw data while the latter focused on events surrounding a crime. Both authors look for relationships between the objects they are examining. The work of (Batten and Pan 2011) extended the work of both Carrier and Marrington by demonstrating how relationships between the objects of investigation could be used to reduce the size of the data set needing analysis (and so speed up the investigation time) and also by developing a visualization technique of the analysis to assist the investigation team.

All of (Carrier 2006), (Marrington 2009) and (Batten and Pan 2011) develop extensive methodologies for relationship building. (Carrier 2006) gives examples of hypotheses which can be formulated and tested; however, he does not attempt to define the word hypothesis in the digital forensic context. The authors of (Al-Zaidy et al. 2012) use a similar method of relationship building to find communities of criminals by examining documents seized from suspect computers. Their Algorithm 2 develops 'hypotheses' in the form of relationships between people and data; however, the authors do not define formally what they mean by a hypothesis.

The contributions of the current paper are: 1) to formally present a definition of hypothesis in the context of digital forensic investigation and 2) to illustrate, via an extensive case study, how our theoretical formulation is able to find relationships from which hypotheses can be developed and examined. The impact of our work is first of all to support the investigation by formalizing a procedure which results in the generation of hypotheses which are most likely to be relevant, and secondly to provide the investigator with a formal process presentable to a court of law on the basis of its scientific approach and reproducibility.

In Section 2, we describe the relevant literature. Section 3 contains formal definitions and notations needed to describe our subsequent work. A case study is presented and then analyzed in Section 4. Finally, in Section 5, we summarize the implications of our work on the future research literature in this area.

2 Related Work

Using the hypothesis generation concept, (Chen 1996) proposes a business intelligence framework to improve fraud detection and intelligence decision analysis. In this framework, each potential hypothesis is subjected to three tests: there is first an adjustment to eliminate anomalies; abductive reasoning is then applied taking the context into consideration and results in adaptation yet again; finally, a conflict resolution model checks for contradictions. Chen's framework works well on a business information system, but is not easily adaptable to a digital forensic investigation involving multiple and variable sources of information.

In medical diagnosis, a medical doctor attempts to determine the actual cause of some symptoms. Much attention has been paid to this in the recent research literature where, for instance, Bayesian network models were applied in (Yang 2010), conformal predictors framework in (Làmbrou et al., 2011), and clustering discrimination in (Chang et al., 2010). In addition, (Webster et al. 2010) propose a hybrid model which combines multiple information sources and improves the quality of the hypotheses generated. However, the above models are not suitable for our research problem for several reasons. Firstly there is usually no tight deadline for results while speedy solutions are often required in a forensic investigation. Secondly, medical models require input of a uniformed set of data in a standardized format, such as blood test data, patient history and so on, while such standardized data is not available in digital forensics. Thirdly, the above models assume that medical data is from reliable sources and can be taken at face value, but digital forensic investigators often encounter data which has been deliberately manipulated to avoid detection or usefulness.

A popular application of hypothesis generation is found in question/answering (QA) games. QA games may ask a question and request an answer, or provide an answer and ask for a question which leads to that answer. For example, IBM's *Watson*, is a sophisticated QA system which generates hypotheses of high quality to pose as questions for a given answer (Ferrucci et al. 2009). Watson parses a given answer into a search tree, generates alternative questions as hypotheses, and looks for possible solutions from a given corpus of data. When Watson finds a candidate question, it assigns a confidence level and retains the question as a possible solution if the confidence level is over a certain threshold (Ferrucci et al. 2010). Similar to Watson, (Chen and Garcia 2010) generates semantically valid hypotheses by assessing the semantic quality of a dataset while (Di Lecce and Calabrese 2012) generates hypotheses based on the observations of automated learning results of applying syntactic pattern recognition. These natural language processing approaches successfully rely on data redundancy and explicit rules in natural languages but less ably handle digital evidence of a great variety of complexity and uncertainty.

Utilizing the finite-state machine concept, (Carrier 2006) proposes that investigators should formulate hypotheses to answer questions about the states of events and verify that observations match actual data. Carrier's approach requires all information and resources relevant to the investigation to be collected and observed. The limitation of this approach is that finite-state machines do not scale well and become error-prone as the volume of evidence increases. In this paper, Carrier does not mention the concept of relationship and its application to hypothesis generation.

In (Marrington 2009), the author proposes an automated process to describe a computer system and its activity for computer forensic investigation. He explains that a computer profile consists of finite sets of objects, relationships, the times in the history of the computer system and the events. This work complements existing activities in digital investigations by producing a formal description of a computer system and facilitates the formulation of hypotheses by the investigator about the computer system's activity (Marrington et al. 2010). The authors of (Batten and Pan 2011) expand on Marrington's work by introducing dynamic object sets and relations which is effective in reducing the otherwise fast growing number of objects. A framework proposed to identify relationships between the members of an email network is presented in (Haggerty et al. 2011) and graph theory is applied to a case study.

While informal use of hypotheses is made in all of these approaches, and each paper argues that hypotheses are necessary, no formal definition of hypothesis generation has been proposed. In Section 3, we provide such a definition.

3 Hypothesis Generation

The starting point for the formal approach to hypothesis generation is based on the work in (Marrington 2009) and (Batten and Pan 2011) and the reader is referred to those papers for more details. We begin with a set of objects **O** which have been collected in the preliminary stage of the investigation; relationships are then established between some of these objects. For instance, given objects *printer* and *computer*, we might establish the relationship that '*the computer is connected to the printer*'. Given those relationships, inferred relationships can then be constructed as in (Marrington 2009).

In our context, **O** is the set of items perceived to be in the vicinity of, or connected to, a forensic investigation. The definitions below are standard definitions used in set theory or the theory of binary relations and can be found in (Herstein 1975).

Definition 1. *A relation **R** on **O** is a subset of ordered pairs of* **O**×**O**.
Definition 2. *A relation **R** on **O** is reflexive if* (a,a) ∈ **R** *for all* a *in* **O**.

We can assume without any loss of generality that any relation on **O** in our context is reflexive since this property neither adds nor deletes information in a forensic investigative sense.

Definition 3. *A relation **R** on **O** is symmetric if* (a,b) ∈ **R** *implies* (b,a) ∈ **R** *for all objects* a *and* b *in* **O**.

Again, without loss of generality, in our context we assume that any relation on **O** is symmetric. This assumption is based on an understanding of how objects in **O** are related. So for instance, a printer and PC are related bi-directionally in the sense that they are connected to each other.

Definition 4. *Given a reflexive and symmetric relation **R** on **O**, for each element* a ∈ **O**, *we define a relational class for* a *by* (a) = {b| (a,b) ∈ **R**, b ∈ **O**}.

Note that, because of reflexivity, a∈**O** is always an element of the relational class (a). Given a set **O** of objects and a relation **R** on **O**, we now define what we mean by a hypothesis on **O** and **R**.

Definition 5. *A **hypothesis** h about **O** and **R** is a statement involving a non-empty subset* O_h *of* **O** *such that for all* a ∈ O_h, *if* $|O_h|$>1, *then there is an element* b ∈ O_h *with* b≠a *such that* (a,b) ∈ **R**.

Thus, in an investigation, hypotheses are generated using objects from a non-empty subset of the object set; if there is more than one object present, then it must be related to some different object also used in the hypothesis. This latter condition forces the investigator to use the defined relationships to generate hypotheses. We need the condition b≠a since we allow the case of a hypothesis about a single object from **O**, and since each object is related to itself because of the reflexive property, Definition 5 could be trivially satisfied for any set of objects whether related or not.

Thus we have introduced an important forensic constraint that hypotheses should be about objects which are related. However, the word 'statement' in the above definition is quite vague; in our context, we mean an English language statement and we give an example below to illustrate this. Note that, for each subset O_h chosen, the set of all hypotheses can be generated algorithmically in finite time since the number of words in English is finite; however, the number is combinatorially large and so impractical to generate in real time.

Notation. Let **R** be a set of relations on the object set **O**. Then **H(O, R)** is the set of all hypotheses which can be generated from **O** and **R** for all non-empty subsets of **O**.

Example. Suppose that {Alice, printer, document} is a subset of **O** and that **R** contains (Alice, printer) and (printer, document). Then the statement: 'Alice printed the document on the printer' satisfies definition 5. The statement 'Alice did not print the document on the printer' is also a valid hypothesis.

Analyzing the hypotheses In order to analyze the hypotheses generated from the sets of objects and relations, the investigator assigns confidence levels to them. While a binary logic would assign only one of two values (1 for true or 0 for false) to a hypothesis, in our case, it is generally not possible to be so precise. The investigator, however, may be able to convince herself, based on the evidence and circumstances, that a particular hypothesis may be 'more true than false' and in this case wish to assign it a value between 0 and 1 but closer to 1, say 0.6 or 0.7 on a spectrum of [0,1]. (See (Gerla, 2001) or (Krantz and Kunreuther, 2007.) We formalize this definition now.

Definition 6. *A **characteristic function** on a set S is a map $c:S \rightarrow [0,1]$. For $x \in S$, we call $c(x)$ the **confidence level** of x with respect to S.*

In case *S* is the set of all hypotheses generated in an investigation, we shall insist on the following: if $h \in H$ is known to be true, then $c(h)=1$; if $h \in H$ is known to be false, then $c(h)=0$. Otherwise, the investigator assigns a confidence level strictly between 0 and 1 to **H**. For practical purposes, we limit the choice of confidence value by using only the values 0, 0.1, 0.2, 0.3,…,1.

Continuing from the ***Example***, if Alice shares the printer in an open office and no evidence suggests that Alice prints the document, then an investigator might assign 0.5 to both hypotheses because she feels there is an equal chance that Alice printed the document. But if Alice confesses to printing the document, then the investigator assigns 1 to the hypothesis "Alice printed the document" and 0 to the complement.

In applying our methodology, based on time and resources, the investigator determines a number of rounds to be run, and in each round will generate a set of hypotheses. We use $H_i = H_i(O_i, R_i)$ to refer to the set of hypotheses generated in round *i* based on object set O_i and relation set R_i. Clearly, $H_i \subseteq H(O_i, R_i)$. Let $U = \cup_i H_i$, the union of the set of hypotheses generated in a fixed set of rounds.

At this point, the investigator needs to make some decisions which we list here.

D1. The investigator assigns a confidence level $c(h)$ to each member h of U.

Let $U^+=\{h \in U$ such that $c(h)>0.5\}$.

D2. (a) If $U^+ \neq \square\square$, then consider extensively the elements of U^+ in order to resolve the investigation. (b) If $U^+=\square\square$, choose a new (larger) bound on the number of rounds and continue until either the bound is reached or $U^+ \neq \square\square$.

D3. If $U^+ = \square\square$ after the rounds and time available have been exhausted, then make changes to the original sets **O** and **R** and repeat the procedure.

In practice, for a large investigation, different sets **O** and **R** can be established initially and the scheme above run in parallel. Our goal is in fact to isolate only those hypotheses in U^+ of specific investigative interest and of high confidence level. We tackle this by re-interpreting the relationship on **O** in a different way from (Marrington et al. 2010).

4 Case Study and Analysis

In order to illustrate our hypothesis generation methodology, we now present a case study which requires all aspects of our theoretical setup. This case study is taken from the earlier work of (Batten and Pan 2011) where it was used to develop the object set and relations developed during a forensic investigation. In this paper, we modify the object and relational development to show how hypotheses can be generated and examined in assisting the investigator to draw some conclusions about the case in reasonable time and with some certainty about the final decisions.

The case is copied here in its original form as follows:

"Joe operates a secret business to traffic illegal substances to several customers. One of his regular customers, Wong, sent Joe an email to request a phone conversation. The following events happened chronologically —

2009-05-01 07:30 Joe entered his office and switched on his laptop.
2009-05-01 07:31 Joe successfully connected to the Internet and retrieved his emails.
2009-05-01 07:35 Joe read Wong's email and called Wong's land-line number.
2009-05-01 07:40 Joe started the conversation with Wong. Wong gave Joe a new private phone number and requested continuation of their business conversations through the new number.
2009-05-01 07:50 Joe saved Wong's new number in a text file named "Where.txt".
2009-05-01 07:51 Joe saved Wong's name in a different text file called "Who.txt".
2009-05-01 08:00 Joe hid these two newly created text files in two graphic files ("1.gif" and "2.gif") respectively by using S-Tools with password protection.
2009-05-01 08:03 Joe compressed the two new GIF files into a ZIP archive file named "1.zip" which he also encrypted.
2009-05-01 08:04 Joe concatenated the ZIP file to a JPG file named "Cover.jpg".

2009-05-01 08:05 Joe used Window Washer to erase 2 text files ("Who.txt" and "Where.txt"), 2 GIF files ("1.gif" and "2.gif") and 1 ZIP file ("1.zip"). (Joe did not remove the last generated file "Cover.jpg".)

2009-05-01 08:08 Joe rebooted the laptop so that all cached data in the RAM and free disk space were removed.

Four weeks later, Joe's laptop was seized by the police due to suspicion of drug trafficking. As part of a formal investigation procedure, police officers made a forensic image of the hard disk of Joe's laptop. Moti, a senior officer in the forensic team, is assigned the analysis task." (*End of case in (Batten and Pan 2011).*)

Moti runs Forensic ToolKit to filter out the files of known hash values from a verified forensic image of Joe's laptop. Then he defines **O** = {250 emails, 50 text files, 100 GIF files, 90 JPG files, 10 application programs} as his initial object set. To avoid analyzing all data bit by bit Moti adopts our hypothesis generation approach which works in multiple rounds. The number of rounds is set by the investigator and possibly adjusted as the investigation proceeds. Moti has two working days before a report is due and decides to try for at least three rounds in the first day and in each round generate hypotheses which satisfy Definition 5.

Round 1 Suspecting that Joe uses the installed programs to process other files, Moti establishes his object set and relational classes as follows: $\mathbf{O_1}=\mathbf{O}$ and $\mathbf{R_1}$ ={(a,b) | a ∈{10 application programs}, b ∈{250 emails, 50 text files, 100 GIF, and 90 JPG files}}on the basis that application programs are indicative of user behavior (Bem and Huebner 2007). Moti's first hypothesis set is $H_1(\mathbf{O_1},\mathbf{R_1})$ = {h_1="Joe used the 10 application programs"}. To validate this hypothesis, Moti establishes that all programs were used in a virtual environment and that the programs S-Tools and WinZip were used frequently.

Round 2 Expecting to see that the visible files are clean, Moti establishes his object set and relational classes as follows: $\mathbf{O_2}$= {250 emails, 50 text files, 100 GIF, 90 JPG files} and $\mathbf{R_2}$={(a,b) | a, b ∈{250 emails, 50 text files, 100 GIF, 90 JPG files}}. Moti's second hypothesis set is $H_2(\mathbf{O_2},\mathbf{R_2})$ = {h_2 = "Joe did not hide information in the object files"}. Moti uses the data carving tool Scalpel but discovers 10 ZIP files each of which is concatenated behind a JPG file.

Round 3 With the newly recovered ZIP files, Moti establishes his object set and relational classes as follows: $\mathbf{O_3}$= {10 newly recovered ZIP files, WinZip program} and $\mathbf{R_3}$= ={(a,b) | a ∈{10 newly recovered ZIP files } and b is the WinZip program} so that he can use WinZip to explore the new files. Moti's third hypothesis set is $H_3(\mathbf{O_3},\mathbf{R_3})$ ={h_3= "Joe hid information in the 10 ZIP files"}. Moti attempts to extract the 10 ZIP files, and finds that they are encrypted.

Moti has now spent a full working day on three rounds and assigns the confidence level $c(h_1)$=1. Moti also sets the confidence levels $c(h_2)$=0 and $c(h_3)$=0.5 since concatenating a file behind a JPG file is a popular and practical anti-forensic method. Then, he reviews U^+ which contains only h_1 and does not help in wrapping up the case. Therefore Moti decides to extend the investigation for another 3 rounds during the second working day.

Round 4 Having decided to use the program PRTK to crack the 10 encrypted ZIP files, Moti establishes the object set and relational classes as follows: O_4={10 encrypted ZIP files} and R_4= {(a,a) | a∈{10 encrypted ZIP files}}. Moti reuses his third hypothesis in the next set: $H_4(O_4,R_4)$ = {h_4=h_3= "Joe hid information in the 10 ZIP files"}. Moti manages to crack the 10 encrypted ZIP files and extract the contents as 20 new GIF files.

Round 5 During tea break, Moti recalls that the program S-Tools is frequently used on Joe's laptop but has not yet been investigated. Furthermore, S-Tools steganographically embeds small text files into GIF files. Hence, he decides to reset the object set and relational classes as follows: O_5= {20 new GIF files, 100 GIF files from Round 1, 50 text files, S-Tools} and R_5 ={(a,b) | a ∈{20 new GIF, 100 old GIF, 50 text files} and b is S-Tools}. Moti's fifth hypothesis is $H_5(O_5,R_5)$ = {h_5= "Joe used S-Tools to hide information as text files in the GIF files"}. Moti tries to manually recover information by using S-Tools, and thus the progress is slow.

Round 6 As an experienced investigator, Moti suspects that Joe might have used some of his personal information to construct passwords and so he adds Joe's personal information to the object set and to relational classes as follows: O_6= {20 new GIF files, 100 GIF files, 50 text files, S-Tools, Joe's personal information} and R_6={(a,b) | a, b ∈{20 new GIF, 100 GIF, 50 text files, S-Tools, Joe's personal information}}. Moti's sixth hypothesis set is $H_6(O_6,R_6)$ = {h_6="Joe used S-Tools to hide information as text files in the GIF files encrypted by his personal information"}. After some trial and error, Moti uses Joe's medical card number to recover two text files from two GIF files. One text file contains the word "Wong" and the other the number "0409267531".

After completing rounds 4, 5 and 6, Moti evaluates his confidence levels. He believes that the information found is related to Joe's alleged drug trafficking business. Moti conservatively sets his new confidence levels to $c(h_4)$=1, $c(h_5)$=1 and $c(h_6)$=1 and decides to extend the investigation to a final round.

Round 7 Moti focuses on the hypotheses and information related to h_4, h_5 and h_6. He adds the new text strings to the object set and relational classes as follows: O_7 = {20 new GIF files, 100 GIF files, 50 text files, S-Tools, Joe's personal information, the two recovered text files, the name Wong, the number 0409267531} and R_7 = {(a,b) | a, b ∈ O_7}. His new hypothesis set is: $H_7(O_7, R_7)$ ={h_7 ="The mobile phone number 0409267531 belongs to Wong", h_8 = "Joe used S-Tools to hide drug-trafficking information as text in GIF files encrypted by his personal information", h_9= "Joe and Wong have a client/customer relationship in selling/buying drugs"}. Moti searches through mobile phone registration directories and finds that the number "0409267531" is registered under the name "Alex Wong" who has been charged with drug possession. Thus, Moti regards "Wong" as a suspect in Joe's drug trafficking case. His confidence levels are $c(h_7)$=1 because the ownership of the mobile phone is confirmed, $c(h_8)=0.8$ because Moti believes that more information remains in the other GIF pictures, and $c(h_9)=0.6$ because Moti needs to investigate how Wong relates to Joe.

It is almost the end of the second working day and Moti writes a case report illustrating his steps in finding the two text strings from the digital items. He suggests that Wong is a suspect in Joe's drug trafficking case and requests more time to further explore his hypotheses in the set $U^+=\{h_1,h_4,h_5,h_6,h_7,h_8,h_9\}$.

In summary, this case study demonstrates the use of hypothesis generation during a digital forensic investigation where many assumptions and decisions are made by investigators. This new approach moves beyond relationship building, already used by several authors, to focus on hypotheses generation which aids investigators to make justified decisions based on identified evidence. The investigator analyzes only those relations and hypotheses about which he is confident and eliminates others.

5 Discussion and Future Work

This paper takes a scientific approach, using formal and systematic methods of building relationships on objects, to the development of hypotheses in a digital forensic investigation. A formal definition of 'hypothesis' is given and applied throughout the procedure which comprises a series of rounds in which relations are built on the objects under investigation from which, in turn, hypotheses are generated. In each round, the object, relation and hypothesis set may change, depending on the results of the previous rounds. Confidence levels are assigned to the hypotheses by the investigator and when the target number of rounds is reached, those hypotheses with sufficiently high confidence levels are analyzed. The case study of Section 4 demonstrates the usefulness of a formal definition of 'hypothesis'.

Because the methodology is highly structured it lends itself to easy adoption by an investigator and also to a semi-automated process which can reduce the investigation time. Since the structure lends itself to reproducibility, the method is particularly appropriate for presentation in a court of law where each round or stage of the process can be examined thoroughly. While the automated nature of our procedure is evident, we have not yet written software to apply to our case study; this is the next step in our work. In addition, we hope to be able to collaborate with a forensic team to test our methodology on a real case.

6 References

Al-Zaidy, R., Fung, B., Youssef A., and Fortin, F. (2012), "Mining criminal networks from unstructured text documents", *Digital Investigation*, vol. 8, no. 3-4, pp. 147-160, Elsevier.

Batten, L.M. and Pan, L. (2011), "Using relationship-building in event profiling for digital forensic investigations", in Lai, X., Gu, D., Jin, B., Wang, Y. and Li, H. (Ed.) *Forensics in Telecommunications, Information, and Multimedia*, vol. 56, pp. 40-52, Springer.

Bem, D. and Huebner, E. (2007), "Computer forensic analysis in a virtual environment", *International Journal of Digital Evidence*, vol. 6, no. 2, 13 pages, Utica College, New York.

Carrier, B. (2006), "A hypothesis-based approach to digital forensic investigations", *CERIAS Tech Report 2006-06,* Purdue University, Center for Education and Research in Information Assurance and Security, West Lafayette.

Chang, J.Y., Huang, Z.C. and Shen, Z.Y. (2010), "Medical Diagnostics System Based on Clustering Discrimination", in *Proceedings of IEEE 2nd International Conference on Information Engineering and Computer Science (ICIECS)*, pp. 1-4.

Chen, F. (1996), *Hypothesis generation for management intelligence*, PhD thesis, Deakin University, Melbourne, Australia.

Chen, P. and Garcia, W. (2010), "Hypothesis generation and data quality assessment through association mining", in *Proceedings of 9th IEEE International Conference on Cognitive Informatics (ICCI)*, pp. 659-666, Beijing, China.

Di Lecce, V. and Calabrese, M. (2012), "Syntactic pattern recognition from observations: a hybrid technique", in *Bio-Inspired Computing and Applications Lecture Notes in Computer Science*, vol. 6840, pp. 136-143, Springer.

Ferrucci, D., Brown, E., Chu-Carroll, J., Fan, J., Gondek, D., Kalyanpur, A., Lally, A., Murdock, J., Nyberg, E. and Prager, J. (2010), "Building Watson: an overview of the DeepQA project", *AI Magazine,* vol. 31, no. 3, pp. 59-79.

Ferrucci, D., Nyberg, E., Allan, J., Barker, K., Brown, E., Chu-Carroll, J., Ciccolo, A., Duboue, P., Fan, J. and Gondek, D. (2009), "Towards the open advancement of question answering systems", *IBM Research Report. RC24789 (W0904-093)*, IBM Research, NY.

Gerla, G. (2001), *Fuzzy logic: Mathematical tools for approximate reasoning*, Springer.

Haggerty, J., Karran, A.J., Lamb, D.J. and Taylor, M. (2011), "A framework for the forensic investigation of unstructured email relationship data", *International Journal of Digital Crime and Forensics*, vol. 3, no. 3, pp. 1-18, IGI Global.

Herstein, I. (1975), *Topics in algebra*. Wiley, New York, 2nd edition.

Jankun-Kelly, T., Wilson, D., Stamps, A.S., Franck, J., Carver, J. and Swan, J. (2009), "A visual analytic framework for exploring relationships in textual contents of digital forensics evidence", in *Proceedings of VizSec, IEEE*, pp. 39-44, Atlantic City, New Jersey, USA.

Krantz, D. and Kunreuther, H. "Goals and plans in decision making," Judgement and Decision Making 2(3):137-168, 2007.

Lambrou, A., Papadopoulos, H. and Gammerman, A. (2011), "Reliable confidence measures for medical diagnosis with evolutionary algorithms", *IEEE Transactions on Information Technology in Biomedicine*, vol.15, pp. 93-99, IEEE.

Marrington, A. (2009), *Computer profiling for forensic purposes,* PhD thesis, QUT, Australia.

Marrington, A., Mohay, G., Morarji, H. and Clark, A. (2010), "A model for computer profiling", in *Proceedings of IEEE International Conference on Availability, Reliability, and Security*, pp. 635-640, Poland.

Webster, Y., Gudivada, R., Dow, E., Koehler, J. and Palakal, M. (2010), "A framework for cross-disciplinary hypothesis generation", in *Proceedings of the 2010 ACM Symposium on Applied Computing*, pp. 1511-1515, Switzerland.

Willassen, S. (2008), "Hypothesis-based investigation of digital timestamps", *International Federation for Information Processing, Advances in Digital Forensics IV*, vol. 285, pp. 75-86.

Yang, Y.P. (2010), "A consistency contribution based Bayesian network model for medical diagnosis", *Journal of Biomedical Science and Engineering*, 3(5), pp. 488-495, Inderscience.

Pypette: A Framework for the Evaluation of Live Digital Forensic Acquisition Techniques

B. Lempereur, M. Merabti and Qi Shi

School of Computing and Mathematical Sciences
Liverpool John Moores University
L3 3AF
e-mail : b.lempereur@2006.ljmu.ac.uk, {m.merabti,q.shi}@ljmu.ac.uk

Abstract

With the increasing scale of digital forensic investigations, there is a need for approaches that are capable of reducing the quantities of data forensic examiners are required to search. As this trend continues, traditional quiescent digital forensic analysis is in some cases becoming impractical; examiners must often rely on an in-situ investigation of the live computing environment. Numerous approaches to live digital forensic evidence acquisition have been proposed in the literature, but relatively little attention has been paid to the problem of identifying how the effects of these approaches, and their improvements over other techniques, can be evaluated and quantified. In this paper, we present Pypette, a novel framework enabling the automated, repeatable analysis of live digital forensic acquisition techniques.

Keywords

Digital forensics, live digital forensics, experimental computer science.

1 Introduction

Scale is a pervasive problem in Digital Forensics. In 1999, McKemmish (McKemmish 1999) published a report for the Australian Institute of Criminology in which he identified the volume of data and prevalence of digital devices as future research issues. More than ten years later, this is still the case (Haggerty & Taylor 2007; Distefano & Me 2008; Richard III & Roussev 2006). The growth in static storage has been "tremendous," and the number of embedded devices that could feasibly be used to participate in crime, often equipped with their own proprietary operating systems, is increasing (Mohay 2005).

Traditional approaches to digital forensic investigation are quiescent, in that they require the examiner to power-off the subject machine and make a bit-for-bit copy of non-volatile storage media before proceeding with any examination (Sammes Anthony & Jenkinson 2007). As the nature and scale of computing systems continues to change this approach is, in some cases, impractical; examiners must often rely on an in-situ investigation of the live computing environment (F Adelstein 2006; Hay et al. 2009).

Live digital forensics presents unique challenges with respect to maintaining forensic soundness, but also offers the ability to examine information that is unavailable to quiescent analysis, namely the operational state of the system. The evidence gained from this approach, however, lacks credibility (Wang et al. 2009). This problem is exacerbated by the possibility of malicious software altering the output from live digital forensic software (Rutkowska 2007). Despite this, there has been no systematic attempt to examine the side effects and accuracy of live digital forensic approaches to evidence acquisition.

We believe that live digital forensic evidence, which describes how a computer was actually used, is a useful addition to inferences drawn from artefacts in documents and files, and that if employed correctly it can be a significant aid to an investigation. In this paper, we propose a novel approach to evaluating the effects and accuracy of live digital forensic acquisition techniques. Where existing approaches have focused on evaluation based on a percentage of memory change before and after acquiring live forensic evidence, we consider the accuracy and effects of methods in terms of the artefacts forensic examiners actually need to extract from systems, and the mechanisms they use for achieving this. The result of this work is Pypette, a framework for performing automated, repeatable experiments on live digital forensic acquisition techniques.

The rest of this paper is organised as follows. General concepts in live digital forensics and initial work towards evaluating live digital forensics are discussed in §2. In §3 we present the design of our live forensic experimentation framework. The results from our implementation and feasibility assessment are given in §4. We conclude the paper in §5 with a summary of our approach and directions for further work.

2 Related Work

When a system cannot be powered off, because of legal, technical, or other reasons, analysts must perform a live forensic analysis. Regardless of whether the examiner is taking a quiescent or live approach, acquiring and analysing evidence in a forensically sound manner is paramount to the success of an investigation and the acceptance of evidence in court. To be considered forensically sound, processes must meet the following criteria (McKemmish 2008):

- The meaning of electronic evidence should not be altered by the process.

- Any errors should be identified and "satisfactorily explained."

- Processes should be available for, and stand up to, independent verification.

- Analysts should have sufficient and relevant experience.

Casey (Casey 2007) states that a puritanical approach to forensic soundness, where any alteration to evidence renders it inadmissible, is unhelpful. When performing a live analysis, the state of a computer is necessarily altered, and this is consistent with other forensic disciplines.

Despite numerous publications, high-profile coverage (Richard III & Roussev 2006; F Adelstein 2006; Carrier 2006; Hay et al. 2009), and proven value (Hargreaves & Chivers 2008; Schatz 2007), the inadmissibility of evidence captured using live techniques remains the prevailing attitude among digital forensic researchers and practitioners (7Safe Information Security 2007). We believe this to be a combination of a social and a technical problem. Until the necessary techniques are developed to allow first-responders, who may not be experts, to perform live analysis it is likely (perhaps reasonable) that the techniques will remain a niche area of digital forensic practice, and consequently research.

The techniques used to acquire artefacts during live forensic analysis will be subject to examination and review when their conclusions are presented in court. Sutherland et al. (Sutherland et al. 2008) conducted an empirical study to determine the impact of live forensic tools on subject systems, using a limited set of measurements, including the amount of memory altered by the live acquisition technique, its impact on the Microsoft Windows environment, and dependency on dynamic libraries.

During their investigation into volatile memory forensics (Walters & Petroni 2007) conducted a very limited analysis of the impact of live memory acquisition tools on Microsoft Windows XP hosts. The decision to measure the effectiveness of memory acquisition tools as a percentage of bytes changed on the system after their execution is short-sighted. Once an image of memory and the page file have been captured, to the extent that the size of the page file is not automatically increased by the operating system, it is inconsequential how much memory is altered during live analysis. Therefore, a reliable way to detect changes would be to compare the system state before imaging with the image captured by the acquisition tool.

A more thorough examination of live digital forensic memory acquisition techniques was presented in (Inoue et al. 2011), using visualisation mechanisms to check for systematic errors. This approach was effective; however, they note a difficulty in obtaining "ground-truth" images of machine state against which to evaluate their method. We aim to address this problem by approaching the evaluation of these techniques as an experiment, using virtualisation to host the testing environment, allowing for the repeatable collection of a ground-truth image from the virtual machine manager.

3 Pypette

Existing research relies on the establishment of, and comparison to, a baseline figure of memory change as a function of time (Walters & Petroni 2007), or counting the number of memory pages altered by the live digital forensic acquisition technique. We believe this view oversimplifies the problem, and that the operational state of a system after acquisition is irrelevant so long as the captured state accurately reflects the original machine before a live digital forensic intervention. Therefore, we propose that a meaningful result can be obtained by viewing the process in terms of the artefacts examiners are attempting to extract using live analysis.

To gain a complete picture of accuracy and effectiveness, these artefacts should be extracted from the state captured by live forensic acquisition and compared to the resulting state of the system, its initial state, and the state the machine would be in had no intervention occurred. Finally, since computer systems are, in practice, rarely deterministic, this comparison should be performed multiple times; statistical analysis of the results will allow us to determine the most likely outcome of different types of acquisition and analysis in various scenarios.

Our goal when creating the framework is to provide a standard set of techniques that will enable experts to quickly design and execute new experiments. Parallel to this, a repository of scenarios for live evidence acquisition, provided as virtual machines, should be developed to allow for comparable results from different evidence acquisition methods. While existing research has shown that achieving this is difficult (Garfinkel et al. 2009), we believe that some degree of commonality between comparisons will be helpful for future live digital forensic research.

For the remainder of this section, we first discuss the implementation of our framework and the interface for implementing experiments. We conclude the section by presenting the mechanism we use to evaluate the accuracy of a live forensic technique, and the effects it has on its environment.

3.1 Conducting Live Forensic Experiments

Pypette is a framework for conducting experiments into live digital forensic acquisition and analysis techniques following the principles outlined above. From a developer's perspective, the framework is structured as three concepts: techniques, actors, and analysts. Experiments are written as Python programs, inheriting behaviour from the framework in a manner that lets developers "pick and choose" the most appropriate technique, actor, and analyst for their scenario, extending the framework where functionality is missing or complicated behaviour desired.

The technique acts as a factory, supplying instances of actors and analysts to the framework that will carry out the majority of the work. They should remain unaware of the specific details of the environment in which they will operate. All a technique need do is to check the feasibility of execution on a specific virtual machine, that is, whether the configuration is sufficient to allow the actor to perform its function without failure, and if the result will be meaningful to the analyst. Actors are responsible for intervening in the execution of a virtual machine, applying a live digital forensic acquisition or analysis technique, and extracting the results onto the host system. Analysts extract artefacts from, and collate the results of, the intervention, which is then fed into a statistical model that determines the accuracy of the technique.

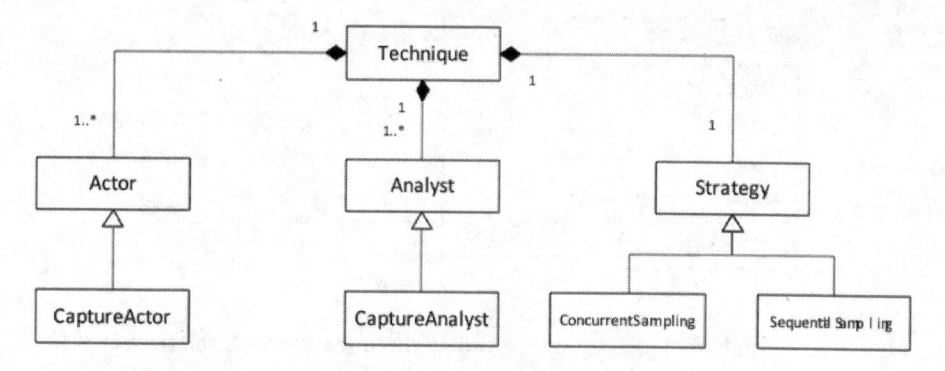

Figure 1: Component hierarchy of the experiment interface.

In our initial work, we assumed that control and live virtual machines should always run in parallel. Asides from more complicated cases where, for example, a suite of virtual machines are used to conduct an experiment, this may not always be the best approach even for single-machine cases. Instead, we allow the developer to determine the appropriate sampling strategy, selecting from a predefined library, or implementing their own where appropriate.

The responsibility of the sampling strategy is to coordinate the sampling of subject and control machines within the overall scope of an experiment. How this is arranged affects the functionality of both actor and analyst, to the extent that some sampling strategies may be incompatible with some techniques. With this in mind, we have provided a general interface for sampling strategies, and implementations of both concurrent and sequential strategies for the single-machine experiment case. This is sufficient for the majority of experiments that we foresee being conducted using the framework. Figure 1 shows the hierarchy that comprises a technique, along with the implementations of actors, analysts, and sampling strategies that are in-place for use by developers.

To provide the emulation platform for our experiments, we use the QEMU virtual machine manager, running in either kernel-assisted full-virtualisation, or user-land emulation modes. A software agent that communicates with the host using the virtual serial port controls actions within the virtual machine. These actions include spawning and capturing the output of processes, locating mounted volumes using a simple UUID-token placed in the root of the file system, and ensuring that correct ejection of removable media.

Figure 2 shows the communication architecture between the Pypette framework, the virtual-machine manager, and the in-host virtual machine agent. All messages between server and client are exchanged using a line-oriented, JSON-based protocol over UNIX domain sockets.

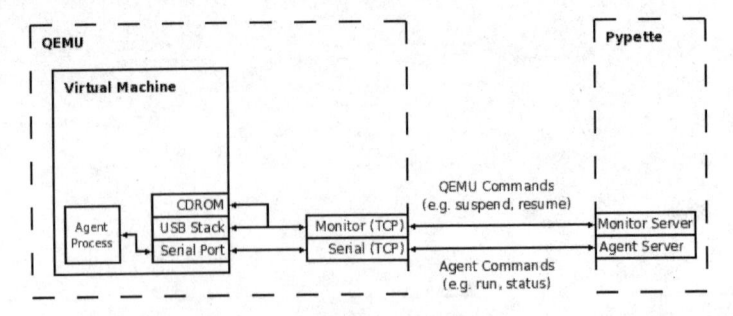

Figure 2: Virtual machine emulation and communication with the framework.

To allow for repeatable experiments, machines are instantiated from an image of their state that has been migrated to a file on disk. A machine state defines the situation for an experiment, and testing a technique in a variety of situations gives an impression of how we can expect it to perform. While a migration image contains the contents of a machine's memory, we must also provide the stored media, namely hard-disk images and removable media that contribute to a situation. For this purpose, we create and use only copy-on-write clones of the exemplar machine's storage, leaving the original media intact. These duplicates are also available for analysis, and in future work we will investigate the application of automated forensic storage analysis techniques to provide further information about the effects of live digital forensic acquisition methods.

3.2 Analysing the Results of Experiments

We employ a novel technique to evaluate the accuracy and forensic soundness of evidence acquisition methods that compares the imperfect, in-situ view available to live digital forensics, against a perfect system-image captured using a virtual machine manager. Figure 3 shows the comparisons we perform, and the information they provide about the live forensic technique. The dashed lines represent the different samples that are taken from the control and subject machines, with arrows indicating the comparison performed between them. By comparing the state of the machine at these three different points, we can:

- Measure the accuracy figure for the live digital forensic acquisition technique, by determining how closely its output reflects the initial state of the system.

- Measure forensic soundness through analysing the state in which the acquisition technique leaves the system, compared to both its initial state and the state it would be in had no intervention occurred.

- Establish a disturbance figure for the virtual machine, had no intervention occurred, a baseline against which we determine the accuracy and forensic soundness of the technique.

By collecting this information from a scripted experiment over a number of iterations, we can build a picture of how we expect a live digital forensic technique to perform in a given scenario.

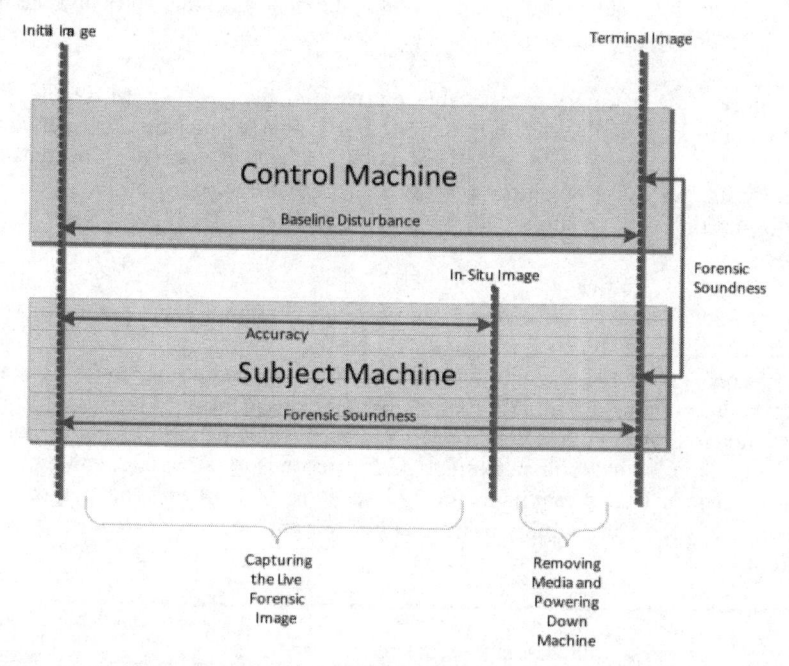

Figure 3: Sampling and analysis strategy for single-machine experiments.

We achieve support for the automated extraction of evidence from acquired memory images through an interface to the Volatility suite of memory analysis techniques. As part of our framework, we use this interface to provide the analysts for single-machine memory and artefact capture techniques. It is also available to developers implementing their own analysts.

4 Results

To determine the efficacy of our approach to live digital forensic experimentation, we designed a small-scale test using the memory acquisition tool "mdd" (ManTech International Corporation 2009). The platform for the experiment was a clean installation of Microsoft Windows XP SP3, on the i386 platform, configured with 1GB RAM, a graphics card, and no networking support. The sampling procedure was:

1. Introduce a copy of the acquisition tool to the subject machine as a CDROM image.

2. Instruct the in-situ agent to execute the capture tool within the subject machine, saving the contents to an additional drive.

3. Suspend the execution of both virtual machines and take the final memory snapshots.

4. Attach the additional drive image to the host machine, and copy the in-situ memory capture to a temporary location.

We selected to examine process table entries and their associated handles in the initial and in-situ captures as, with the machine being isolated from the network, we expected to see the highest degree of volatility in these areas. To analyse the memory images captured during the experiment, we developed an extension to the single machine capture analyst that exported results to JSON documents for later study.

The technique behaved consistently across the 211 samples we gathered, with no significant differences in machine state between experiment iterations. Table 1 shows an overview of the number of processes and handles gathered from each sample. It is interesting to note that the number and identity of processes remained constant across all samples, with a relatively small fluctuation in their associated file handles. Experiments took an average of 256 seconds to complete, with a minimum of 186 seconds, and a maximum of 329 seconds. Given that the purpose of the experiment was as a feasibility assessment of our approach, we believe this outcome is promising.

	Mean Processes	Min Processes	Max Processes	Mean Handles	Min Handles	Max Handles
Initial	21	21	21	4397	4397	4397
In-Situ	66	66	66	4578	4566	4588
Control	21	21	21	4305	4190	4370

Table 1: Presence of process table entries and their associated file handles in memory images, with the in-situ image extracted using "mdd" (n = 211).

There is insufficient space in this paper to present the results in full; however, we intend to publish further examinations of live digital forensic techniques, particularly those relating to memory extraction, in addition to examining the effects of turbulent, network connected, and malware-infected environments.

5 Conclusions and Further Work

In this paper, we have presented Pypette, a novel framework enabling the automated, repeatable analysis of live digital forensic acquisition techniques. Where existing approaches have focused on evaluation based on a percentage of memory change before and after acquiring live forensic evidence, we consider the accuracy and effects of methods in terms of the artefacts forensic examiners actually need to extract from systems, and the mechanisms they use for achieving this. Initial results have shown that our framework is capable of conducting repeatable experiments and generating consistent results.

In future work we will refine the model used to analyse the results of live digital forensic acquisition, in addition to providing further templates to ease the process of designing experiments for our framework. Parallel to this, we will conduct a series of experiments on various live digital memory acquisition techniques in the presence of turbulent, networking connected, and malware-infected environments.

We also intend to investigate the possibility of extending the framework to provide a training platform for first-responders. It would be possible to allow the user to interact with the live machine, either providing an interface to interact with machine hardware, or directly attaching devices from the host to the guest machine. Scripted training sessions would allow the collection of detailed metrics regarding user-performance and the accuracy of collected evidence.

6 References

7Safe Information Security, 2007. Good Practice Guide for Computer-Based Electronic Evidence.

Adelstein, F, 2006. Live forensics: diagnosing your system without killing it first. Communications of the ACM, 49(2), p.66. Available at: http://portal.acm.org/citation.cfm?id=1113034.1113070.

Carrier, B.D., 2006. Risks of live digital forensic analysis. Communications of the ACM, 49(2), pp.56–61. Available at: http://portal.acm.org/citation.cfm?id=1113034.1113069.

Casey, E., 2007. What does "forensically sound" really mean? Digital Investigation, 4(2), pp.49-50.

Distefano, A. & Me, G., 2008. An overall assessment of mobile internal acquisition tool. Digital Investigation, 5, pp.121–127. Available at: http://linkinghub.elsevier.com/retrieve/pii/S174228760800042X.

Garfinkel, S. et al., 2009. Bringing science to digital forensics with standardized forensic corpora. Digital Investigation, 6, p.S2-S11. Available at: http://linkinghub.elsevier.com/retrieve/pii/S1742287609000346 [Accessed August 4, 2011].

Haggerty, J. & Taylor, M., 2007. FORSIGS: forensic signature analysis of the hard drive for multimedia file fingerprints H. Venter et al., eds. New Approaches for Security, Privacy and Trust in Complex Environments, 232, pp.1–12. Available at: http://www.springerlink.com/index/21478KR877478805.pdf.

Hargreaves, C. & Chivers, H., 2008. Recovery of encryption keys from memory using a linear scan. In Proceedings of the 2008 Third International Conference on Availability, Reliability and Security. IEEE Computer Society, pp. 1369–1376. Available at: http://portal.acm.org/citation.cfm?id=1371602.1371819.

Hay, B., Bishop, M. & Nance, K., 2009. Live Analysis: Progress and Challenges. IEEE Security and Privacy, 7(2), pp.30–37. Available at: http://www.computer.org/portal/web/csdl/doi/10.1109/MSP.2009.43.

Inoue, H., Adelstein, Frank & Joyce, R. a., 2011. Visualization in testing a volatile memory forensic tool. Digital Investigation, 8, p.S42-S51. Available at: http://linkinghub.elsevier.com/retrieve/pii/S1742287611000302 [Accessed August 4, 2011].

ManTech International Corporation, 2009. MDD Physical Memory Acquisition. Available at: http://sourceforge.net/projects/mdd/.

McKemmish, R., 1999. What is forensic computing. Trends and Issues in Crime and Criminal Justice, 118. Available at: http://aic.gov.au/documents/9/C/A/{9CA41AE8-EADB-4BBF-9894-64E0DF87BDF7}ti118.pdf.

McKemmish, R., 2008. When is Digital Evidence Forensically Sound? Advances in Digital Forensics IV, pp.3–15. Available at: http://www.springerlink.com/index/048J747850234355.pdf.

Mohay, G., 2005. Technical challenges and directions for digital forensics. In Systematic Approaches to Digital Forensic Engineering, 2005. First International Workshop on. pp. 155–161. Available at: http://scholar.google.com/scholar?hl=en&btnG=Search&q=intitle:Technical+challenges+and+directions+for+digital+forensics#0.

Richard III, G.G. & Roussev, V., 2006. Next-generation digital forensics. Communications of the ACM, 49(2), p.80. Available at: http://portal.acm.org/citation.cfm?id=1113074.

Rutkowska, J., 2007. Beyond the CPU: Defeating hardware based RAM acquisition. Proceedings of BlackHat DC 2007. Available at: http://lollobox.org/lollobox/raw-attachment/wiki/TheProject/DoesntProtectFrom/bh-dc-07-Rutkowska-up.pdf.

Sammes Anthony, J. & Jenkinson, B., 2007. The Treatment of PCs. In Forensic Computing. London: Springer, pp. 277-299.

Schatz, B., 2007. BodySnatcher: Towards reliable volatile memory acquisition by software. Digital Investigation, 4, pp.126-134. Available at: http://www.citeulike.org/user/jksahani/article/6863807.

Sutherland, I. et al., 2008. Acquiring volatile operating system data tools and techniques. ACM SIGOPS Operating Systems Review, 42(3), pp.65–73. Available at: http://portal.acm.org/ citation.cfm?id=1368516.

Walters, A. & Petroni, N., 2007. Volatools: integrating volatile memory forensics into the digital investigation process. Black Hat DC. Available at: http://scholar.google.co.uk/scholar?q=volatools&hl=en&btnG=Search&as_sdt=2001&as_sdtp=on#0.

Wang, L., Zhang, R. & Zhang, S., 2009. A Model of Computer Live Forensics Based on Physical Memory Analysis. In 2009 First International Conference on Information Science and Engineering. IEEE, pp. 4647-4649. Available at: http://ieeexplore.ieee.org/xpl/freeabs_all.jsp?arnumber=5454440 [Accessed August 8, 2011].

On Dimensions of Reconstruction in Database Forensics

O.M. Fasan and M.S. Olivier

ICSA, Computer Science, University of Pretoria, South Africa
e-mail: mfasan@cs.up.ac.za, molivier@cs.up.ac.za

Abstract

Although very little amount of research has been done on database forensics, current research has tacitly focused on digital examination and reconstruction of databases from a number of dimensions. The general assumption is that only one of these dimensions needs to be handled during database forensics investigations. This paper analyses the dimensions in which research in database forensics has been focused on and uses these to reveal the different aspects of database forensics which are yet to be explored. The paper also elaborates on the tools and techniques currently being used in database forensics analysis process and highlights some of the challenges being faced in database forensics research and practice as they relate to the dimensions implied by current research in database forensics.

Keywords

Database forensics, Digital examination, Reconstruction, Forensics analysis.

1 Introduction

Database systems have become a core component of many computing systems and are often used to store critical and sensitive information relating to an organization or her clients. Unfortunately, the increase in the usage of databases to store volumes of information together with the increased relevance of the data on many databases in solving crimes have led to an increased number of attacks on databases and interests in investigating databases for artifacts that may assist in solving different crimes.

Database forensics is an emerging branch of digital forensics that deals with the identification, preservation, analysis and presentation of evidence from databases (Fowler, 2008). Although digital forensics has grown over the last decade from a relatively obscure trade-craft to an essential part of many investigations (Garfinkel, 2010), the same cannot be said of database forensics. Despite the large amount of research that has been done on digital forensics, database theory and database security, very little has been done on database forensics (Olivier, 2009) even though investigations involving databases have been explored in theory and practice.

Database forensics research has taken various directions as more researchers explore the field. Even though there is currently no defined underlying model for database forensics, the dimensions in which research has taken are worth exploring. The aim of this paper is to reflect on the research in database forensics and expose the directions in which research has been focused as well as how these directions relate to each other. The paper shows how the research directions form a basis for future research in database forensics and highlights the drawback in the structure of the research directions. The currently available tools for database forensics as they relate to these research directions as well as the techniques that should be employed in database forensics in general are described in the paper. An overview of the challenges being faced in database forensics research and practice are also discussed.

2 Database Forensics

Until recently, traditional digital investigations often excluded databases even though evidence can usually be found in them. Although the field is still in its early years, it is quickly becoming an important part of many investigations due to the increased volume of information that may be helpful in solving different crimes and the large number of risks associated with the information stored on many databases.

Of major importance in database forensics is the ability to retrace the operations performed on a database and reconstruct deleted or compromised information on the database. This requirement affects how data is collected and analyzed during the forensics analysis of a database. Although different aspects of database forensics have been explored by researchers over the past few years, the research works have taken directions that define various dimensions of reconstruction and investigation in database forensics. An inspection of these dimensions shows the research that has been done in relation to each dimension and reflects some of the aspects of database forensics that is yet to receive any research attention.

3 Dimensions of Reconstruction in Database Forensics

The little database forensics research that has been done seems divergent, often focusing on aspects that may only be relevant in a fraction of forensic investigations of databases. We argue that these apparently diverging strands of research are, in fact, related. More than that: we argue that they form different dimensions of a problem space, where most work done until now have focused on a specific dimension of this space. By realising that the individual contributions address a single dimension of a larger space, it becomes possible to focus on the larger problem by considering situations that involve more than one dimension. The following dimensions emerge from the literature:

1. Compromised database.
2. Damaged database.
3. Modified database.

Below, each of these dimensions is considered in more detail and illustrated by positioning previous research (from multiple authors) into a dimension. After that, we proceed to show that scenarios that entail more than one dimension are, in fact, likely and thus substantiate our claim that the database forensics problem is indeed multidimensional. Our conjecture, based on current research publications, is that the problem space will be three dimensional.

3.1 Research on Compromised Databases

We define a compromised database as a database where some of the metadata or some software of the database management system (DBMS) have been modified by an attacker even though the database is still operational. A major concern of database forensics in this situation is that an investigator cannot trust the information provided by the database being investigated. Olivier (2009) pointed out that although a database itself seems to be the best tool for collecting data for forensics analysis, the integrity of the data contained or the results obtained from queries cannot be trusted since the database might have been coerced into giving false information, for example, if the data dictionary has been modified. The problem was also identified by Litchfield (2007d) while discussing steps to perform in a live response to attack on an Oracle database. Beyers et al. (2011) consider four abstract layers of a DBMS and investigate various techniques that can be used for data collection when one or more abstract layers have been compromised. The major decision that has to be made when investigating a compromised database is whether to use the metadata as it occurs on the database being investigated or to try to get a clean copy of the DBMS.

3.2 Research on Damaged/Destroyed Databases

In contrast to compromised databases, the category of damaged or destroyed databases refers to databases where the data contained or other data files may have been modified, deleted or copied from their original locations into other places. These databases may or may no longer be operational depending on the extent of the damage done. Most of the research in database forensics falls into this category.

The series of papers by Litchfield (2007a; 2007b; 2007c; 2007e; 2007f; 2008) describe practical methods for recovering data from an Oracle database using different data sources on the database. Wright (2010) also explained technical methods for identifying when the data on an Oracle database has been modified and how to recognize vulnerabilities in the database. In his book on SQL server forensics, Fowler (2008) discusses the effects which database rootkits can have on the collection and analysis of data from a SQL server database. The book also highlights steps to be followed when database rootkits are detected.

Other research which falls into this category deals with the detection of database tamper, and data hiding in a database. Snodgrass et al. (2004) proposed a technique which relies on cryptographically strong one-way hash functions for detecting when the data on a database has been tampered with. Their idea was extended to deal with the forensics analysis of a data security breach in a subsequent paper by Pavlou and Snodgrass (2006), where the notion of corruption diagrams was introduced as a way of visualizing attacks and forensic analysis algorithms. Another algorithm for detecting tampering and determining what and when a database was tampered with was also presented by Pavlou et al. (2010). Although the work of Stahlberg et al. (2007) and that of Pieterse and Olivier (2012) seem to be anti-forensics, they both expose the areas in a database that should be checked for previously deleted data or any form of information hiding on a database during forensics analysis.

Proceedings of the Seventh International
Workshop on Digital Forensics & Incident Analysis (WDFIA 2012)

In order to investigate a damaged database, it may be necessary to employ techniques in file carving (Carrier, 2005) in regenerating destroyed files or underlying files in a database which may helpful in retrieving data of interest.

3.3 Research on Modified Databases

We refer to a modified database as a database which has not been compromised or damaged but has undergone changes due to normal business processes since the event of interest occurred. This category of databases is often of interest when a database is not directly involved in the crime being investigated but is used to store information that may assist in solving other crimes. Fasan and Olivier (2012) examine how the information in a database at an earlier time can be reconstructed even though several modifications of the data might have occurred. The authors introduced the notion of relational algebra log, value blocks and inverse relational algebra. The proposed reconstruction algorithm works by traversing the query log and performing series of forward or backward (inverse) queries on relations in the database based on the value blocks. In general, there are various locations where forensic data can be found on a database, especially in compromised or damaged databases. A brief overview of these locations is discussed in section 5.2.

3.4 Orthogonality of the Reconstruction Dimensions

At the moment, research in database forensics treats the dimensions discussed above as being orthogonal. Figure 1 shows the positioning of previous research in database forensics into a single dimension of the database forensics problem space.

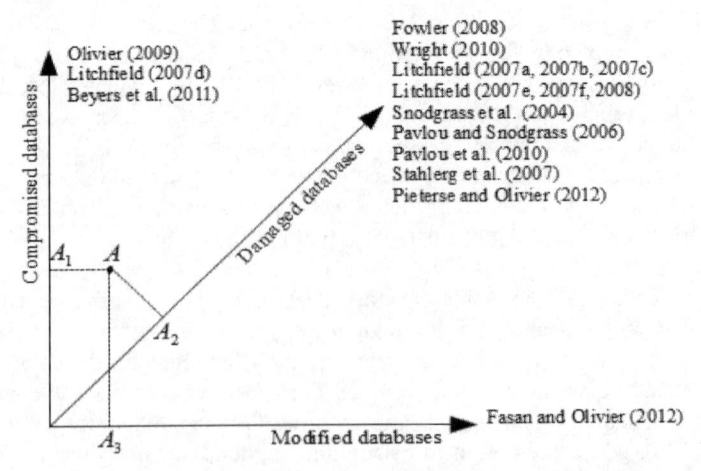

Figure 1: Dimensions of Database Forensics

We posit that a database being investigated may belong to one or more dimensions with varying degrees. For example, an investigation may be positioned at point A on this space (figure 1), such that the database being investigated has been compromised at A_1 degrees, damaged at A_2 degrees and modified at A_3 degrees. Thus, it is possible that someone compromises a database by modifying the metadata and then later destroys some of the data on the database in order to hide traces of the compromise. The database forensics problem space is at least three dimensional, with any given investigation positioned somewhere in this three dimensional space. This poses not only a research challenge, but also a challenge in practice: one may need heuristics during an investigation to determine where in this space to start the investigation. Moreover, it also raises questions about whether or not it is possible to quantify the degree of each dimension that occurs when investigating a database and the order to be followed in investigating each possible dimension. In deciding the techniques to be used in any investigation, we propose that questions relating to the trustworthiness of a database, the presence and/or authenticity of the data it contains and modification of the database should first be asked and investigation should be conducted in each dimension while putting into account the degree of that dimension. For example, if we are at the origin of the three dimensions (that is, where the database has not been compromised, damaged or modified) then data can be collected by simply querying the database but the same approach will not be applicable when the database has been compromised and/or damaged. Since there is no defined method for identifying a compromised database, it may be better to assume that we are at the origin of these dimensions when investigating time or mission critical databases and then make educated guesses from possibly contradictory information gathered based on the initial assumption.

The decision regarding the dimensions to be considered in an investigation and extent or degree of each dimension determines the tools that should be used, as well as the process that should be followed during a database forensics investigation.

4 Database Forensics Tools

The unavailability of tools for database forensics is a reflection of the little amount of research that has been done in the field. Database forensics tools should allow information from different sources on a database to be gathered and assist in investigating and recovering of information regardless of the dimensions involved in the investigation. They should also be able to determine when a database has been compromised or damaged. Currently, database forensics is done with tools which are not designed for forensics analysis or with the database system itself, through the query processor. Thus, most of the tools being used are only applicable to specific database management systems and are focused on investigating damaged databases. Quite a number of research are also on-going on the development of new tools.

Although many of the tools being used for database forensics have been helpful for collecting data and identifying transactions that indicate fraudulent activities, most of these tools are not accurate or precise enough to be used as a forensics tool. For example, the Oracle LogMiner was investigated for possible use as a forensics tool by Wright (2005). He reported that there are anomalies with the way it works which makes it inadequate for a forensics analysis. Other tools that have been used include audit features such as the SQL Server Audit and the Oracle Audit.

The database itself is also used as a forensics tool (Olivier, 2009) because it enables an investigator to search the data it contains using powerful queries. However, the database cannot be used as a tool to investigate itself when dealing with a compromised database as one is instantly faced with questions about the integrity of the database and how to ensure that the database has not been coerced into giving false result, for example, if the data dictionary has been modified. Moreover, the query processors on many databases often optimize queries in ways that cannot be controlled by the user. An investigator has to be certain that an optimized query is an exact representation of the original query, especially when dealing with damaged databases where data files on the database might have been modified. These constraints restrict the use of databases as a forensics tool for itself in many cases.

As the field of database forensics develops further, it is hoped that more tools specifically designed for the forensics analysis of databases will be developed. Litchfield (Westervelt, 2007) announced that he is in the process of developing an open source tool called Forensic Examiner's Database Scalpel (FEDS) for database forensics a few years ago. Some of the major concerns that may be faced in the development of tools include the fact that the data model is typically hardcoded into database management systems and since such model that can be used as a forensics tool for itself does not currently exist, new models will have to be created (Olivier, 2009). Thus, more research is still required in order to develop tools that are specifically designed for database forensics. The development of these tools calls for an understanding of databases as well as the processes involved in database forensics analysis. In the following section, we describe the database forensics process and techniques applicable in various stages of the process.

5 Database Forensics Process

Research in digital forensics has led to the development of various techniques and process models. However, many of these techniques are not completely transferable to database forensics due to certain characteristics of databases which require them to be adapted for handling database forensics. This section discusses some of the techniques in digital forensics as it applies to database forensics analysis.

5.1 Data Acquisition and Preservation in Database Forensics

The acquisition of data from a modified database that has not been damaged or compromised is often done by simply querying the database. However, when investigating a database that has been compromised and/or damaged, there are three data collection methods that can be used: Live acquisition, Dead acquisition or Hybrid acquisition (Fowler, 2008). As with digital forensics in general, a live data acquisition occurs when the system being analyzed is still running while the analysis is being performed. The dead acquisition method involves copying of data from the system being investigated without using the system itself while the hybrid data acquisition method combines the key elements of both live and dead acquisition methods. Regardless of the method used, it is important to ensure that digital evidence is preserved and data is not unintentionally altered or destroyed.

The objective of the preservation phase is to reduce the amount of evidence that may be overwritten. Extreme care must be taken to guarantee that actions performed do not unintentionally alter data. Although data can be acquired from a modified database by querying the database, the execution of any query that can delete the information on the database must be avoided. Furthermore, no SQL statements should be executed in the case of a compromised or damaged database, regardless of the data acquisition method used as this will modify the data stored in memory and on the database data pages. It may also force internal data page split and the storage of new data in the caches, thus complicating the investigation process.

5.2 Collection and Analysis of Artifacts in Database Forensics

Forensic data often exists in several places on a database. It is important to know which data are important and prioritize evidence collection due to the volatility of some data. Apart from the data which can be collected from a modified database by executing queries, data can also be found in tools normally used by database systems, for example, in the execution plan cache and the transaction logs. An execution plan is a documentation of the most efficient way to execute data requests issued by database users and are stored in the plan cache for possible reuse. The plan cache can be used to identify database misuse by an insider or data damage on a database. The transaction logs help to determine previously executed queries on the database and this is often helpful in various investigations.

Other sources of forensics data in databases consist of files storing histories relating to the database. Some of these files are specifically reserved for the database, for example the database log file and data files while others such as the web server logs and the system event logs of an operating system are not explicitly reserved for the database server usage. It is important to consider the level of volatility of a file when deciding which data to collect first. Fowler (2008) gives a summary of the level of volatility of the various areas in which forensic data can be found on a database.

The analysis of collected data depends on the type of data, the specific DBMS and the specific situation being investigated. The analysis stage should take into account the dimensions involved in any particular investigation and where related information can be found. Another important criterion of the analysis phase of database forensics, is that previously deleted of modified data should be recovered and the actions performed by an intruder must be determined, particularly when investigating compromised or damages databases. The following section describes the steps that should be taken during database forensics investigations in general.

5.3 Database Forensics Investigation Process

There is currently no defined process model for database forensics. The available methods are focused on specific DBMSs. Wong and Edwards (2005) presented a patent method for the forensics analysis of an Oracle database. The method consists of generic steps that a forensic investigator may try to follow to discover more information about an operation that was performed on a database (Olivier, 2009).

Another methodology focused on a damaged SQL server database was presented by Fowler (2008). The methodology consists of four major steps: investigation preparedness, incident verification, artifact collection and artifact analysis.

Although the exact steps to be taken during database forensics will depend on the specific situation and DBMS being investigated, we propose that the database forensics investigation process should in general include the following steps:

a) Determining whether a database has been compromised, damaged or modified, or if an investigation involves more than one dimension; b) determining which acquisition method is most applicable; c) collection of volatile artifacts; d) Collection of non-volatile artifacts; e) preservation and authentication of collected data; f) analysis of collected data and determination of the intruder's activities; g) reconstruction of the database. Some of the various challenges involved in carrying out these steps and in database forensics research in general are discuss in section 6.

6   Challenges in Database Forensics

This paper reveals the lack of extensive research on many aspects of database forensics, which can be attributed to the different challenges involved in database forensics investigations. Olivier (2009) identified three dimensions in which a database needs to be considered during a forensics analysis. This inherent multidimensional nature and complexity of databases that is not yet completely understood in a forensics sense is a major contribution to this lack of research.

In addition, there are various challenges involved in data collection and analysis. First, is how to determine whether a database has been compromised, damaged, modified or has to be handled in more than one dimension. There is no heuristic on where to start an investigation in this three dimensional space. Moreover, deciding the degree of the dimensions involved in an investigation and the most appropriate data acquisition method in investigations with more than one dimension is a challenge since no research which offers a guideline has been done. Another challenge often encountered in database forensics is in the large volume of data that can be collected from a database. An examiner must determine which data are pertinent to an investigation in order to reduce the data set. The process of eliminating some data sources poses challenges such as the misinterpretation or over-interpretation of data due to the number of different file formats in various databases, resulting in the potential dismissal of valuable contents (Cohen, 2006). The information contained in some files is also sometimes encrypted.

Lastly, there is need for the development of a formal model for the reconstruction phase of database forensics, that can be applied regardless of the dimensions involved in an investigation. Also, since reconstruction may involve the recovery of data from proprietary formats, adequate vendor support is required (Olivier, 2009). Collaboration between researchers and database vendors is also required in order to have a good knowledge of the proprietary formats in individual database management systems and aid the development of database forensics tools.

7 Conclusion

Database forensics is still a new research area with very little research and few or no tools. The paper discusses the different dimensions in which database forensics research has been tacitly focused. It also shows that even though these dimensions are currently being addressed as being orthogonal, they should be treated as different dimensions of a single problem space. The paper raises some of the questions that need to be addressed when dealing with multiple dimensions in an investigation. An overview of tools, processes and challenges involved in database forensics research and practice, as well as the need for more research and development of tools which are not dependent on a specific DBMS are also discussed in the paper.

As future work, we plan to investigate the process of reconstructing information in compromised and damaged databases. Various scenarios of investigations involving more than one dimension of the database forensics problem space will be examined. The techniques to be employed during such investigations will also be explored.

8 Acknowledgement

This research was supported by the Organization for Women in Science for the Developing World (OWSD).

9 References

Beyers H., Olivier M., and Hancke G. (2011), "Assembling metadata for database forensics". In proceedings of IFIP international conference on digital forensics, pp.89-99.

Carrier, B. (2005), *File system forensic analysis,* Addison-Wesley Professional, Upper Saddle River, NJ, ISBN: 0321268172.

Cohen, F. (2006), "Challenges to digital forensic evidence", Fred Cohen and Associates. http://all.net/Talks/CyberCrimeSummit06.pdf, (Accessed 20 January 2012).

Fasan, O. M. and Olivier, M. S. (2012), "Reconstruction in database forensics", Presented at the IFIP WG 11.9 International Conference on Digital Forensics, South Africa.

Fowler, K. (2008), *SQL server forensic analysis,* Addison-Wesley Professional, Upper Saddle River, NJ, ISBN: 0321533208.

Garfinkel, S. L. (2010), "Digital forensics research: The next 10 years", *Digital Investigation,* Vol. 7, Supplement, pp.S64-S73. The proceedings of the tenth annual DFRWS conference.

Litchfield, D. (2007a), "Oracle forensics part 1: Dissecting the redo logs", NGSSoftware. www.databasesecurity.com/dbsec/dissecting-the-redo-logs.pdf, (Accessed 17 Feb. 2012).

Litchfield, D. (2007b), "Oracle forensics part 2: Locating dropped objects", NGSSoftware. www.databasesecurity.com/dbsec/Locating-Dropped-Objects.pdf, (Accessed 17 Feb. 2012).

Litchfield, D. (2007c), "Oracle forensics part 3: Isolating evidence of attacks against the authentication mechanism", NGSSoftware. www.databasesecurity.com/dbsec/Investigating-Authentication-Attacks.pdf, (Accessed 17 February 2012).

Litchfield, D. (2007d), "Oracle forensics part 4: Live responses", NGSSoftware. www.databasesecurity.com/dbsec/LiveResponse.pdf, (Accessed 17 February 2012).

Litchfield, D. (2007e), "Oracle forensics part 5: Finding evidence of data theft in the absence of auditing", NGSSoftware. http://www.databasesecurity.com/dbsec/ OracleForensicsPt5.pdf, (Accessed 17 February 2012).

Litchfield, D. (2007f), "Oracle forensics part 6: Examining undo segments, flashbacks and the Oracle recycle bin", NGSSoftware. www.databasesecurity.com/dbsec/oracle-forensics-6.pdf, (Accessed 17 February 2012).

Litchfield, D. (2008), "Oracle forensics part 7: Using the Oracle system change number in forensic investigations", NGSSoftware. www.databasesecurity.com/dbsec/oracle-forensics-scns.pdf, (Accessed 17 February 2012).

Olivier, M. S. (2009), "On metadata context in database forensics", *Digital Investigations*, Vol. 5, No. 3-4, pp.115-123.

Pavlou, K. and Snodgrass, R. T. (2006), "Forensic analysis of database tampering". In proceedings of the 2006 ACM SIGMOD conference on management of data, pp.109-120.

Pavlou, K. and Snodgrass, R. T. (2010), "The tiled bitmap forensic analysis algorithm", *IEEE Transaction on Knowledge and Data Engineering,* Vol. 22, pp.590-601.

Pieterse, H. and Olivier, M. S. (2012), "Application of data hiding techniques in a database environment", Presented at the IFIP WG 11.9 inter. Conf. on digital forensics, South Africa.

Snodgrass, R. T., Yao, S. S. and Collberg, C. (2004), "Tamper detection in audit logs". In proceedings of the 30th inter. conf. on very large databases - volume 30, pp.504-515.

Stahlberg, P., Miklau, G. and Levine, B. N. (2007), "Threats to privacy in the forensic analysis of database systems". In proceedings of the 2007 ACM SIGMOD international conference on management of data, pp.91–102.

Westervelt, R. (2007), "Black hat 2007: New database forensics tool could aid data breach cases", http://searchsecurity.techtarget.com/news/article/0,289142,sid14_ gci1266525,00.html. TechTarget, (Accessed 7 January 2012).

Wong, D. M. and Edwards, K. B. (2005), "System and method for investigating a data operation performed on a database", Number 2005028918, United States patent publication.

Wright, P. M. (2005), "Oracle database forensics using LogMiner", NGSSoftware, www.databasesecurity.com/dbsec/OracleForensicsUsingLogminer.pdf (Accessed 5 February 2012).

Wright, P. M. (2010), *Oracle Forensics: Oracle Security Best Practices*, Rampant Techpress, Kittrell, NC, ISBN: 0977671526.

Assessing Forensic Readiness

A. Chryssanthou[1] and V. Katos[2]

[1]Hellenic Data Protection Authority, Greece
[2]Information Security and Incident Response Unit,
Democritus University of Thrace, Greece
e-mail : achrysanthou@dpa.gr, vkatos@ee.duth.gr

Abstract

In this paper we argue that optimization in terms of forensic readiness should be performed in a controlled and structured manner, taking under consideration the current situation an organization is in. We reflect upon well known practices relating to process maturity and investigate the feasibility and appropriateness of adopting such approaches in order to express forensic readiness. Levels of forensic readiness are defined by using a 0 to 5 scale. By using a fictitious example of an organization's website, which suffers a security breach, we examine how forensically ready the organization is. From this exercise we conjecture that an organization cannot develop or adopt solely generic forensic readiness assessment practices, but there is a need for tailoring.

Keywords

Capability maturity model, forensic readiness

1 Introduction and motivation

Forensic readiness refers to the ability to optimize the forensic processes, which in turn is quantitatively expressed as maximizing the ability to collect digital evidence effectively and minimizing the costs for forensic acquisition and analysis. In the literature we can find suggestions and recommendations for achieving forensic readiness (see for example Rowlingson, 2004). However, these are merely lists of steps that cannot always be applied in practice as the majority of these do not cater for the particular environment they are supposed to operate in. In other words, forensic readiness recommendations are rather "wish lists", where in the absence of a roadmap it is not clear for the organisation on how they can be achieved.

In this paper we argue that in order to start considering forensic readiness, the organisation would need first to have a framework for assessing their current situation. We reflect upon the capability maturity paradigm and express forensic readiness in terms of maturity. By doing this, we inherit the principles, concepts and dynamics of capability maturity which are more appropriate for modelling and expressing processes. We use a fairly common and popular web incident case study as means to validate and evaluate our proposal.

2 The assessment framework

Process maturity is a well established concept in software engineering and this is captured in the widely accepted SEI's capability maturity model, CMM (Paulk et al, 1993). CMM has been ported to the secure systems domain by the International Systems Security Engineering Association and is published as the Systems Security Engineering – Capability Maturity Model, SSE-CMM (ISSEA, 1999). The main focus of capability maturity is on process improvement, and this makes it suitable for adoption in a forensic readiness context. More specifically, forensic readiness is about maintaining processes and technologies for minimising losses and costs during a security breach, with an emphasis on effectiveness of the incident response and digital forensics processes. Against the above it can be easily seen that forensic readiness may be measured against a maturity scale similar to the one provided by SEI.

A core concept used in implementing a maturity model is the so called Process Area (PA) which refers to a defined set of related process characteristics, which, when performed collectively, can achieve a defined purpose. In the case of the SSE-CMM these processes are security engineering related processes. In a similar manner, we define forensic readiness CMM PAs as follows:

Definition 1. A Process Area in a forensic readiness CMM is a defined set of forensic readiness related process characteristics, which, when performed collectively, can achieve a defined purpose.

Identifying PAs in digital forensics is not a particularly challenging exercise because the forensics discipline itself relies on well defined processes. Therefore by leveraging the generic phases of a digital investigation, we perform a straightforward map between these phases and the underlying PAs:

PA01: Identification
PA02: Acquisition
PA03: Examination
PA04: Analysis
PA05: Reporting

With regard to incident response, the PAs are expected to be more pluralistic in nature since we need to include business continuity and disaster recovery practices. The PAs involved are the following:

PA06: Monitoring. This refers to the capabilities and sensors the organisation has in place for capturing, storing and processing data that may be relevant after a security incident takes place.

PA07: Detection. Detection refers to the ability of interpreting the captured data and associating them with a security incident event in a timely manner. Metrics for detection are accuracy and timeliness.

PA08: Response. As soon as a security incident is detected and identified, response covers the escalation processes and decision making for containing the threat, and limiting the negative impact.

PA09: Restore. As soon as the threat is identified and contained, restore processes involve the removal of this threat and the complete recovery of the system to a secure state.

Along with the PAs a maturity model requires a set of generic and base practices. The generic practices are practices that apply to all processes under a specific capability level, whereas the base practices are the PA specific. The ACPO guidelines for example can be adopted as generic practices. In Table 1 a first attempt to define the forensic readiness levels in terms of maturity is presented. This will be refined after applying and studying the case study that is analyzed in the next section.

Forensic Readiness Level	Key Characteristics - examples
0	No log files, hard disks need to be analyzed, no record of normal operation, limited knowledge of web site contents and structure
1 – Initial	Out-of-the-box security (existing default log files, no monitoring), no record of normal operation, adequate knowledge of web site contents and structure
2 – Repeatable	Existing incident handling procedure, applied after incident, no monitoring, just auditing, adequate record of normal operation, full knowledge of web site contents and structure
3 – Defined	Monitoring, Auditing, proactive incident handling, full record of normal operation, full knowledge of web site contents and structure
4 – Managed	Fully defined monitoring and auditing process, being able to answer the question if a packet is normal, if there is an attack and, if so, if the attack is successful or unsuccessful
5 - Optimizing	Not waiting for an attack, monitoring failures, able to filter out failures, honeypots usage

Table 1: Representative forensic readiness levels

3 An example scenario

3.1 Company X

A fictitious commercial **company X**, which sells auto parts, has a website, which is hosted on a web server running Microsoft Internet Information Services 6 and utilizing Microsoft Sql Server as its database server. The website hosts advertising content and contains a clients' area, where **X**'s clients can register to place orders.

Content-wise, the website is based on a custom-made Content Management System (CMS), which was designed by **company A**. The CMS uses ASP to construct dynamic pages, while the website' content is uploaded to the CMS by **A**'s employees by means of FTP. **Company A** is also responsible to correct any obvious programming faults. Nobody has performed any vulnerability testing on the website to find existing security holes, which would make the website prone to web attacks. No record of normal operation exists, in a sense of knowing what traffic the website expects to receive and what constitutes potentially malicious traffic.

On the server side, the website is hosted and supported by **company B**. **Company B** is responsible for applying patches, taking backups and ensuring that the web server is up and running 24 hours a day. The server is protected by a firewall and is accessible by the outside world only through HTTP, FTP and RDP. Auditing is enabled by means of log files, which were by default activated during the installation (out-of-the-box security). However, nobody is monitoring the log files, in order to detect any security incidents.

3.2 The incident

X's website was live for almost 4 years, when it was attacked and compromised by unknown hackers. The attack was not identified in its' reconnaissance stage, when the attackers gathered as much information as possible regarding their target (open ports, running processes, domain contact info, web server and database server editions, structure of website, etc.). Consequently, when the attack eventually succeeded, the attackers managed to steal **X**'s clients' database and post it on the web bragging about their achievement. The attacker's post was uploaded on the web approximately one month after the attack. In the meantime, X did not suspect that the website has been breached. It took three days for X to react to the attacker's post by calling a digital forensics expert to investigate.

3.3 The forensic acquisition

The forensic expert that X hires, being the first responder, makes a first assessment of the situation and proposes the following possible courses of action (Chryssanthou A. and Apostolakis I., 2006):

- X's web server is shutdown and goes offline for a period of at least a week in order for its hard disk to be forensically cloned and examined. Log files from the firewall must be also examined, in case they might also reveal evidence on the attack. As soon as the forensic examination is concluded the company must take appropriate security measures based on the examination findings to correct the security pitfalls that lead to the successful web attack. Additionally, the company will decide on how to handle the examination findings regarding occurred damages.
- X's web server stays online but monitored carefully. In this way, the attackers' activity can be carefully monitored and a more accurate estimate of the damage might be possible. However, it is possible that the attackers

may have had finished their activities. If that is the case staying online would only set the company's transactions in danger by allowing open security holes to stay open and potentially being exploited by other attackers, who have learned about the breach through the original attacker's post on the web. Already, other malicious users have successfully exploited the already open security holes and caused even more damage. Log files must be gathered and forensically analyzed in order for the forensic expert to draw a first conclusion on the web attack incident.

- Digital evidence is collected from X's web server based on order of volatility. X's web server is shutdown and goes offline for a period of at least 6 hours in order for its hard disk to be forensically cloned. Subsequently, the web server is restored from backups dating before the incident and the company takes appropriate security measures to minimize the damage and prevent any future web attacks. However, if the real date of the successful web attack is earlier than the alleged date of the incident, this might pose the risk of restoring an already compromised web server.

The company's management examines the situation and the expert's proposals and votes for option 3. X's management decides to restore a backup, which was taken before the security incident (1 month and 7 days old). In the scale "value of investigation versus continuity of operation" continuity of operation weighs heavier. It is also deemed that the website cannot only stay offline for a period of 4 hours, which does not allow forensic acquisition of the server's hard drive. The expert collects logs from the web server (e.g. IIS simple, IIS advanced logs) and the database server (e.g. current, win security logs), which go back four months before the alleged date of the successful attack, in order to conduct his investigation, along with other volatile data (existing security measures, identification methods, etc.).

3.4 The forensic analysis

The forensic expert maintains a clean forensic copy of the acquired evidence in a secure location and starts his analysis. The point of the analysis is to identify: a) when the breach occurred, b) what method the perpetrator used, c) which security fault lead to the breach, d) which data was extracted.

At first, he loads the log files in automated log analyzers (ManageEngine Event Log Analyzer, Deep Log Analyzer), in order to perform a first assessment of the evidence and decide how to proceed with his investigation. His impression is that company X was receiving for the whole time period, which the log files cover, a series of malicious visits. These visits were not limited in X's country of origin but covered a global scale. The malicious visitors were attempting to break the website's security by means of path traversal, sql injection, cross-site scripting, remote_file_inclusion, local file inclusion and cgi_scripting attacks. A number of web requests indicated the usage of hacking tools such as Zmeu (Theta, 2011; The Linux Page, 2010) and Havij. A number of web requests of hacking tool Havij (HTTP status code 200[1]) was successful.

All log files are imported and analyzed in Microsoft Access 2007 environment. In order to understand each and every log file the forensic analyst has to understand the log formats that IIS and Sql Server use. IIS logs follow the W3C Extended Log File Format (Microsoft, 2012).

The forensic expert has neither a record of how the breached site normally operated nor, due the dynamic nature of the website, any adequate knowledge of web site contents and structure. Thus, he handles the acquired logs as a "black box". He has to make the logs as meaningful as it gets. It can be seen that poor incident detection and response levels (PA07=1, PA08=1) directly affects the analysis, despite a potential high expertise the analyst may have, which is evident from the actions described below.

Firstly, he translates fields, such as *sc-status* (Microsoft, n.d.) to the equivalent message that the system returns (e.g. an HTTP status codes equal to 302 means that the requested object has been moved). He uses as a mean of a translation internal tables which contain the system messages based on type of system and error code (e.g. FTP error codes (Eggleston S., n.d.), IIS status codes, Windows 32 Status Errors (Microsoft, 2011)) and specific web resources on sql server error codes contained within cs-*uri-query* field (Adopenstatic, n.d.). **Secondly**, he downloads an up-to-date ip-to-country open-source database (Maxmind, n.d.), in order to be able to match each visitor's IP to originating country. **Thirdly**, he builds a bot function, which allows him to identify whether a visitor's IP address is blacklisted in Sans Internet Storm Center (https://isc.sans.edu/ipinfo.html?ip="X.X.X.X") by dividing the visitors' IP address in batches of 200 IPs and using the InternetExplorer Visual Basic Object (Microsoft, n.d.) to automate the visits to Sans Internet Storm Center. In this way, the forensic expert builds a table that shows him for every visitor the originating country, if he has been reported for suspicious behavior before and how many times.

Having identified the website visitors, the forensic expert examines the actions which result to a 200 HTTP status code, in order to obtain an image of the website structure as well as the web traffic it receives. Upon examining "200" HTTP Status codes, he comes across a strange finding as shown in the log analysis excerpt (Table 2). This can be captured with the following context related question.

Why should a dynamic page hosting auto parts details answer successfully to requests relating to pharmaceutical products (Viagra, Ampicillin)?

cs-method	cs-uri-stem	cs-uri-query	sc-status	Sc-status_Description	sc-substatus	sc-win32-status	Sc-win32-status_Description	Part Id	Medicin

---

[1] We define as successful a request, which, based on the acquired log file, returned an HTTP Error Code with value 200. We could say that successful are also those requests, which returned an HTTP Error Code with value 500, bur revealed to the attackers, through the accompanying error message, (as stored in IIS log field cs-uri-query), information such as sql server version, table names, etc.

cs-method	cs-uri-stem	cs-uri-query	sc-status	Sc-status_Description	sc-substatus	sc-win32-status	Sc-win32-status_Description	Part Id	Medicin
GET	/store/auto-parts/details.asp	part_id=1342&ampicillin	200	OK. The client request has succeeded.	0	0	The operation completed successfully.	1342	ampicillin

Table 2: A partial view of IIS_Advanced log (1 entry) – Last 2 columns divide the cs-uri-query-field to database id (Part Id) and associated medicine

The investigator calls **company B** and enquires on dynamic page "/store/auto-parts/details.asp". He is provided with a copy of the table "Autopartsdetails" (table that hosts all auto-parts displayed by the before-mentioned dynamic page), where he discovers that:

- Almost 500 illegitimate entries, corresponding to 500 *part_id* ids, have been added in a 3 year period. All of them seem to point to medicines and all of them contain obfuscated code, which, if de-obfuscated (Table 3) corresponds to code reported by the security company Imperva as *"exploiting a Flash vulnerability to install malware"* (Imperva, Contos B., Beery T., 2010).

- All legitimate entries for each part_id have been tampered to include references to the illegitimate ones.

Having found an unexpected second security incident he begins to analyze other HTTP requests (failed and successful) to identify the breach he was called to investigate. Firstly, he excludes "normal" traffic. Afterwards, he records the older security incident that concerned the illegitimate entries and the associated "malicious" content hosted in the table "Autopartsdetails". He then uses attack signatures[2] associated to web attacks (sql injection, path traversal, cross-site scripting, remote file inclusion, etc.) to locate successful web attacks. In order to reduce the amount of log entries he has to examine, the investigator takes a calculated risk and excludes known bots such as MsnBot and GoogleBot, while examining potentially malicious bots (eg. MJ12bot) in groups by identifying them through their User Agent. During his analysis, he realizes that the site was susceptible to sql injection. The website returned errors, pointing to sql injection vulnerabilities, even when **company A** uploaded normal content to the website, errors, which were ignored by company A's employees. The investigated security breach occurred by means of sql injection using Havij 20 days before the hackers posted info of the hack on the web. Having identified the modus operandi of the perpetrator, the time of the breach as well as the security fault which lead to the breach, the investigator needs to establish which data was extracted. In order to identify the extracted data, the investigator needs to decode the sql injection strings which the perpetrator used, which were encoded in URL and ASCII encoding. He has to decode the sql injection strings in order to be able to view them in a humanly

---

[2] See: http://www.neurofuzz.com/modules/software/wsfuzzer/All_attack.txt

comprehensible format and understand which sql commands the perpetrator executed on the on the website's database. In order to perform the decoding he constructs 2 functions which decode the URL encoding of the sql injection string and subsequently, having revealed the second layer of encoding – ASCII encoding, decode the 2nd layer of encoding also (Table 4). In the end it is proven that the entire clients' database of company X was stolen during the breach.

Part Id	Record
1342	1342;1;;;;;2009-07-13 00:00:00.000;"<SCRIPT>document.write(unescape('<S\103R\111PT%3E f\146=0\073 f\0456Fr(\156n%20in%20\144%6Fcu%6Den\04574) \151\146%28nn\075=%27e\164\157%75r\163\047\174\174\156\0456E%3D=\ 047\154og\0456F- a\0456Eim\047\051\040ff\0453D1;\040i\146(f\146%3D\0750\174](\057\0454 CIV\105|M%53N|%59A\110%4F%4F|%43LO\116ID%49%4E\105/.%74\145 s\164%28\144\157cu\0456D%65nt\056re\04566er\04572er\056to%55\04570p e\162%43as\04565()%29%26\04526%66al\04573e\051)\04520d\0456Fcu%6 Den\04574.\167\162i\164\145(%27<\04553C%52IP\04554\040SR%43%3D% 22ht\164\160:%2F\057\160%3090\0453303%2Ein%66%6F/%77.\160h\04570 ?%6C=\047\053e\04573c\141pe%28I\0456F\143at\151on%2E\150re\146)%2 B%27\046k\075\047+e%73ca%70e(%27\04563\154on%69d%69%6Ee\047)+\ 047\046\04572=\047+e\04573\143a%70e(\144oc\165m%65\0456Et.\162ef\04 565%72r\04565r\04529+%27\042>%3C%27\053\047/S%43RI\04550%54>\0 47);\040d\0456F%63um\145nt\0452Ew%72\04569%74e\050%27\074%27+\0 47%21-\055\047)\073 \074\057SC\122\111\120\04554>')) </SCRIPT><TITLE>Ampicillin</TITLE><H3> Ampicillin </H3> *Ampicillin is an antibiotic in the penicillin group of drugs. It fights bacteria in your body. Ampicillin is used to treat many different types of infections caused by bacteria, such as ear infections, bladder infections, pneumonia, gonorrhea, and E. coli or salmonella infection.* -->";;NULL;89;1;0;0;;http://malicioussite.com/	Obfuscated code
1342	1342;1;;;;;2009-07-13 00:00:00.000;" <SCRIPT> ff=0; for(nnin document) if(nn=='etours'||nn=='logo-anim') ff=1; if(ff==0||(/LIVE|MSN|YAHOO|LEVOFLOXACIN/.test(document.referrer.to UpperCase())&&false)) document.write('<SCRIPT SRC="http://p090303.info/w.php?l='+escape(location.href)+'&k='+escape('lev ofloxacin')+'&r='+escape(document.referrer)+'"><'+'/SCRIPT>'); document.write('<'+'!--'); </SCRIPT><TITLE>Ampicillin</TITLE><H3> Ampicillin </H3> *Ampicillin is an antibiotic in the penicillin group of drugs. It fights bacteria in your body. Ampicillin is used to treat many different types of infections caused by bacteria, such as ear infections, bladder infections, pneumonia, gonorrhea, and E. coli or salmonella infection.* -->";;NULL;89;1;0;0;;http://malicioussite.com/	De-Obfuscated code

Table 3: Pharmaceutical malicious entries in table "Autopartsdetails": Obfuscated and De-obfuscated code derive from: Imperva, Contos B., Beery T., 2010, while the Ampicillin definition derives from: NIPA, 2004

cs-uri-query	Decoded cs-uri-query (URL Encoding)	Decoded cs-uri-query (URL & Ascii Encoding)
id=999999.9+UNION+ALL+SELECT+%28SELECT+TOP+1+char%28126%29%2bchar%2839%29%2bcast%28autopartsclient+as+nvarchar%284000%29%29%2bchar%2839%29%2bchar%28126%29+FROM+%28SELECT+TOP+1+autopartsclient+FROM+CLIENTS+order+by+1+asc%29+sq+order+by+1+desc%29%2C0x31303235343830303536[3]%2C0x31303235343830303536%2C0x31303235343830303536%2C0x313032353438303303536%2C0x31303235343830303536%2C0x31303235343830303536%2C0x3130323535343830303536--	id=999999.9 UNION ALL SELECT (SELECT TOP 1 char(126)+char(39)+cast(autopartsclient as nvarchar(4000))+char(39)+char(126) FROM (SELECT TOP 1 autopartsclient FROM CLIENTS order by 1 asc) sq order by 1 desc),0x31303235343830303536,0x31303235343830303536,0x31303235343830303536,0x31303235343830303536,0x31303235343830303536,0x31303235343830303536,0x31303235343830303536--	id=999999.9 UNION ALL SELECT (SELECT TOP 1 ~+'+cast(autopartsclient as nvarchar(4000))+'+~ FROM (SELECT TOP 1 autopartsclient FROM CLIENTS order by 1 asc) sq order by 1 desc),0x31303235343830303536,0x31303235343830303536,0x31303235343830303536,0x31303235343830303536,0x31303235343830303536,0x31303235343830303536,0x31303235343830303536--

Table 4: An attacker's sql injection uri-query in encoded and decoded format

The attack, that lead to the breach, is the first one that successfully extracted data from table CLIENTS, company X's clients database. However, subsequent attacks also extracted data. The investigator cannot establish the extent of these extractions because he has no access to the un-patched site (site before restoring the backup and patching any security holes) in order to check what data were extracted, for example, from system backup tables, etc.

4 Findings

From the above scenario we distilled a number of assessment questions that can be asked in order to create the forensic readiness profile of the organisation, with respect to their web services. These questions and their relation to the respective process areas are shown in Table 5.

From the narrative in Section 3 and by attempting to answer the questions in Table 5, we obtain the forensic readiness profile of the company (Table 6).

---

[3] This string is characteristic of Havij traffic (see: http://lists.emergingthreats.net/pipermail/emerging-sigs/2010-November/010732.html)

Question	PA01: Identification	PA02: Acquisition	PA03: Examination	PA04: Analysis	PA05: Reporting	PA06: Monitoring	PA07: Detection	PA08: Response	PA09: Restore
1. Is it sufficient to examine only log files in case of a security breach?	✓		✓						
2. What would the organisation do if a prior incident was detected during the investigation?						✓	✓		
3. How confident are you with respect to the data integrity of the evidence?		✓							
4. Having only log files, which analysis methodology is to be used? Is there a list of keywords predefined, or is it easy to define the list for the specific context/application?				✓					
5. How would the analysis be differentiated if you had the whole disk image?	✓	✓	✓	✓	✓				
6. If a known published blocked IP (e.g. by SANS) is observed, how certain are you that this IP was conducting an attack?			✓	✓			✓	✓	✓
7. If the log files contain allegedly malicious bot visits, will they be blocked? What incident analysis processes are in place?						✓	✓		
8. How do you analyse obfuscated code? Is there a sterile environment in place?				✓					
9. If company X hosts the services of company Y and the development and support of the code was outsourced to company Z, who is responsible in an event of an sql injection attack?								✓	✓
10. What triggers are in place for detecting sql injection attempts and what escalation procedures are in place?						✓	✓		
11. If company Z discovers sql injection vulnerabilities, what should their course of actions be?							✓	✓	✓

Table 5. Generated assessment questions

5. optimizing									
4. managed									
3. defined			■						
2. repeatable		■		■	■	■			■
1. initial	■						■	■	
	PA01:Identification	PA02:Acquisition	PA03:Examination	PA04:Analysis	PA05:Reporting	PA06: Monitoring	PA07: Detection	PA08: Response	PA09: Restore

Table 6. The forensic readiness CMM of company X

5 Conclusions

We argue that forensic readiness can be better handled with a capability maturity approach. Given that forensic readiness is about minimising costs of conducting a forensic investigation, it is reasonable to argue that a "one size fits all" approach will not be optimum, if it is not adopted in the organisation in question. As such, the process of improving the forensic readiness seems a more suitable solution.

By using a fairly common and popular web incident case study, we demonstrated the applicability of the proposed framework. We observed that assessing the maturity of the organisation in terms of forensic readiness is a more realistic exercise than setting hard targets and goals and expecting an organisation meeting these goals whilst ensuring minimum costs. The questions used to evaluate the maturity are applicable to web incidents. For future work the framework should be expanded to accommodate other types of incidents (such as data exfiltration through social engineering, insider attacks, and so forth).

6 References

Adopenstatic, n.d., "Troubleshooting 80040e14 errors", Available at: http://www.adopenstatic.com/faq/80040e14.asp

Carbonel, J.-C. (2008), "Assessing IT Security Governance Through a Maturity Model and the Definition of a Governance Profile", Information Systems Control Journal, Vol.2, pp1-4.

Chryssanthou A., Apostolakis I., (2006), "Network Forensics: Problems and Solutions", Proceedings of 2nd Conference on Electronic Democracy, Electronic Democracy: Challenges of the Digital Era, Athens Chamber Commerce and Industry.

Eggleston S., n.d., Common FTP Error Codes, Available at: http://www.theegglestongroup.com/writing/ftp_error_codes.php

Havij v 1.15 Advanced Sql Injection Tool, Available at: http://www.itsecteam.com/en/projects/project1.htm

Imperva, Contos B., Beery T., 2010, "Staring at the beast", RSA Conference 2010, Available at: http://www.imperva.com/resources/adc/pdfs/rsa_2010_staring_at_the_beast__6_months_of_attack_vector_research.pdf

International Systems Security Engineering Association, ISSEA, (1999), Systems Security Engineering Capability Maturity Model, Model Description Document. Available at: http://www.sse-cmm.org/model/model.asp

Maxmind, n.d., "Geolite Country – Open Source IP Address to Country Database", Available at: http://www.maxmind.com/app/geoip_country

Microsoft, n.d., "InternetExplorer Object", Available at: http://msdn.microsoft.com/en-us/library/ie/aa752084%28v=vs.85%29.aspx

Microsoft, 2011, "Description of Microsoft Internet Information Services (IIS) 5.0 and 6.0 status codes", Available at: http://support.microsoft.com/kb/318380/en-us

Microsoft, 2011, "Error Messages", Available at: http://msdn.microsoft.com/en-us/library/aa385465%28v=vs.85%29.aspx

Microsoft, n.d., "Log File Formats in IIS (IIS 6.0)", Available at: http://www.microsoft.com/technet/prodtechnol/WindowsServer2003/Library/IIS/bea506fd-38bc-4850-a4fb-e3a0379d321f.mspx?mfr=true

NIPA (National Information Program on Antibiotics), 2004, "Antibiotic Drugs", Available at: http://www.antibiotics-info.org/antibiotic-drugs.html

Paulk, Mark C.; Weber, Charles V; Curtis, Bill; Chrissis, Mary Beth, 1993, "Capability Maturity Model for Software, Version 1.1". Technical Report (Carnegie Mellon University / Software Engineering Institute). CMU/SEI-93-TR-024 ESC-TR-93-177.

Rowlingson, R., 2004, "A Ten Step Process for Forensic Readiness". International Journal of Digital Evidence, Vol. 2, no. 3, pp.1-28.

Theta, 2011, "ZmEu", Available at: http://theta.tk/wiki/ZmEu

The Linux Page, 2010, "Attack By Zmeu", Available at: http://linux.m2osw.com/zmeu-attack?utm_source=[deliciuos]&utm_medium=twitter

A Model for Hybrid Evidence Investigation

K. Vlachopoulos, E. Magkos and V. Chrissikopoulos

Department of Informatics, Ionian University
Plateia Tsirigoti 7, 49100, Corfu, Greece
e-mail: {kostasv, emagos, vchris}@ionio.gr

Abstract

With the advent of Information and Communication Technologies, the means of committing a crime and the crime itself are constantly evolved. In addition, the boundaries between traditional crime and cybercrime are vague: a crime may not have a defined traditional or digital form since digital and physical evidence may coexist in a crime scene. Furthermore, various items found in a crime scene may worth be examined as both physical and digital evidence. In this paper, a model for investigating such crime scenes with hybrid evidence is proposed. Our model unifies the procedures related to digital and physical evidence collection and examination, taking into consideration the unique characteristics of each form of evidence. Our model can also be implemented in cases where only digital or physical evidence exist in a crime scene.

Keywords

Physical forensics, digital forensics, crime investigation models

1. Introduction

Crime is an undisputable part of every society. During the centuries crime has been developed and so did crime investigation techniques. In the 20th century the need for investigating crime in a more accurate way has introduced forensic science, focusing on the collection and examination of evidence connected to a crime. In the 80's-90's the proliferation of computing and Internet technologies has broadened the means of committing a crime. Nowadays, the majority of conventional crime investigations face the need to search for extra evidence that may have been stored in digital form or been produced by digital devices. For example, offenders of the -so called- traditional crimes, like homicides or rapes, may have used the Web, e-mail, or cellular communication services to collect and transfer information related to the crime. Examining this evidence can for example produce valuable information about a crime, the motives of the offenders, the relationship between the offender and the victim, the accomplices of the offender. As a result, digital forensics flourished, becoming the key player in the battle against crime. (Reith et al., 2002; Palmer, 2002; Vlachopoulos, 2007; Beebe, 2009; Garfinkel, 2010; Agarwal et al., 2011).

In this cyber-physical environment it becomes extremely difficult to collect every single scratch of evidence or to find a specific piece of evidence. In the digital investigation field for example, a number of challenges need to be studied and addressed (Sheldon, 2005; Beebe, 2009; Garfield, 2010), including: The decreasing size of storage devices which makes the creation of a forensic image or the processing of the data they contain, challenging; the expansion of malware stored in RAM that demands the development of specialized RAM forensics tools; the proliferation of smartphones and pervasive computing technologies that extend the need to search for evidence in a variety of new digital devices or physical items with embedded systems-on-chip (SOC), *e.g.*, clothes; the use of cloud computing technologies so that evidence cannot be found in a single computer or network and may be stored and/or processed outside the legal jurisdiction; legal issues related to security and privacy that influence both physical and digital investigation and the admissibility of collected evidence.

The growing role of digital evidence to support conventional criminal evidence also illustrates the need for law enforcement agencies to adopt new investigation methods. Up to now, most investigation models deal with only physical or only digital evidence, thus imposing a clear separation. For example U.S. National Institute of Justice (2000) manual about the crime scene investigation and Lee's *et al.* (2001) Scientific Crime Scene Investigation Model do not include specifications about digital evidence and their role in the documentation of a case. Even the U.S. National Institute of Justice Special Report for electronic crime scene investigation (2008), focuses mainly on procedures concerning digital devices and not on the interpretation of the data they contain. On the other hand, state-of-the-art digital forensic models do not sufficiently pay much attention to physical evidence which is also very important for a case. (Palmer, 2001; Carrier and Spafford, 2003; Ciardjuain, 2004; Rogers *et al.*, 2006; Agarwal *et al.*, 2011; Yusoff *et al.*, 2011).

We believe there is often a constant interaction between digital and physical evidence in a crime scene and novel investigation strategies should be pursued, aiming to avoid the loss of crucial evidence, physical or digital. For example, if an operating computer is used only as a source of physical evidence (for example fingerprints), there is the danger of losing volatile data or terminating a running process by an accidental move of the mouse or a keystroke. On the other hand if a computer is faced only as a source of digital evidence it is possible to miss physical evidence like fingerprints and DNA which could be collected from the surface or the internal of a computer or peripheral device. Furthermore, various items found in a crime scene may worth be examined as both physical and digital evidence *e.g.*, a printed paper which can be related to a specific printer, personal computer, flash memory etc, or a piece of clothes with an embedded system-on-chip (SOC) which may contain important data about the case under investigation. Clearly, dealing with hybrid evidence in a crime scene requires law-enforcement agencies to use a combination of physical and digital forensics methods and techniques.

Our Contribution. In this paper we propose a model for hybrid evidence investigation where both digital and physical evidence may co-exist in a crime scene. The novelty of the proposed model is that we do not discriminate between physical and digital evidence investigation, but instead we consider all evidence types potentially present in most crime investigations. Our model extends the traditional physical crime scene investigation models which law enforcement agencies use for decades to incorporate the digital environment. An important feature of the model is that it can also be used in crime scenes where only digital or physical evidence exist.

2. Related work

Crime investigation theory remains an open field of research as offenders find new ways to commit crimes. In law enforcement investigations, commonly accepted procedures are implemented by most agencies around the world. For instance a typical investigation includes the following basic steps (Vlachopoulos, 2007): Police are notified about a crime; after the necessary preparation an investigation takes place at the crime scene; the scene is secured, a thorough search for evidence is contacted and items considered as evidence are documented, bagged, labeled, collected and transported to the lab for further examination; finally a police report refers to the results of the investigation.

The majority of models that have been presented so far for physical crime scene investigations include a number of common steps. For example, the U.S. National Institute of Justice report on Crime Scene Investigation (2008) includes nine top level steps: a. Preparation, b. Preservation, c. Preliminary Documentation and Evaluation of the scene, d. Documentation, e. Collection, f. Preservation, g. Package, h. Transport, i. Report. These steps are met in most investigation models.

Lee *et al.* (2001) presented the *Scientific Crime Scene Investigation Model*, which focuses on a systematic and methodical way of investigating a physical crime scene. Although the model refers only to physical crime scene investigation, it became a point of reference as many of its aspects can be used to search for digital evidence in an electronic crime scene investigation. The model refers only to the forensic part of an investigation, while issues such as preparation and exchange of information with other investigators are not addressed.

In the *Digital Forensic Research Workshop* (Palmer, 2001), a digital forensic investigation model was suggested which includes a set of seven steps derived from a number of actions that have to be performed in each step. The aim of the model was to set the basis for future work which would define a full model. It became a point of reference in the coming years as its steps are included in most of the recent models. The model cannot be used directly in a real investigation as it does not include a comprehensive explanation of the actions that have to be performed in each step but only a list of overlapping techniques.

Carrier and Spafford (2003) suggested a digital investigation process, which includes both physical and digital evidence investigation in one integrated process. The model consists of seventeen phases organized into five groups. The basic characteristic of the model is the separation of the investigation process to physical and digital crime scene investigation. Firstly, items found in the crime scene are handled as physical evidence using traditional investigation methods (*e.g.*, fingerprints). If these items are source of digital evidence (*e.g.*, computers, cellphones, peripherals) they are examined again according to digital crime scene investigation sub-phases and the results are added to the primary physical scene. The main disadvantage of this approach is that the time needed to collect physical evidence could lead to loss of volatile data or other digital evidence related to the crime.

Ciardjuain (2004) evaluated and combined the existed models to propose the *Extended Model of Cybercrime Investigations* which consists of thirteen steps. Unlike previous models, it includes steps and processes before and after the crime scene investigation. The sequence of steps in the model is not absolute. Some steps can be omitted, their sequence can be modified and the results from a step can influence not only the next step but the previous one as well. The sequence of the activities described in the model could contribute to the development of new tools for digital evidence examination. The model only refers to digital evidence.

The *Computer Forensics Field Triage Process Model* (Rogers et al., 2006) aims to identify, examine and interpret digital evidence as soon as the investigation begins, without the need to take the evidence to the lab for further examination. The model focuses on the need to collect as much evidence as possible, immediately after the investigation begins as in many cases immediate action is required to resolve the crime. The model also focuses on the specifics of each case *e.g.,* investigating child pornography is different than investigating drug activities or financial crimes. This feature limits the model's value since it can be used only in a limited number of cases. Furthermore, the format of the model resembles to a computer-based or network-based forensic model, where physical evidence is totally ignored.

The *Systematic Digital Forensic Investigation Model* (Agarwal et al., 2011) includes eleven stages which are similar to the ones that had been suggested in previous models, except the evidence collection stage which is divided into Volatile Evidence and Non-Volatile Evidence Collection sub-phases. It is a comprehensive model, targeting computer frauds and cyber crimes investigations. Basically, the model ignores the physical nature of evidence. Only the Non-volatile evidence collection sub-phase considers evidence of non-digital nature such as written passwords, hardware and software manuals, related documents and computer printouts. Critical physical evidence like fingerprints or DNA which could be found on the surface or the internal of the devices placed at the crime scene, are ignored.

Recently, Yusoff et al. (2011) presented an assessment on digital investigations models, from 1985 to 2011. They examined the existed models and determined their common phases. These common phases were used to make the *Generic Computer Investigation Model* which consists of five generic phases. The five generic phases which are included in the model represent the main phases of each investigation in a physical or digital crime scene. Their model seems more like a framework than a model, since its phases are too general to be implemented ad hoc in a real world investigation process.

Table 1, presents the top level phases of a selection of state-of-the-art investigation models and the target evidence of each model (physical or digital) is highlighted.

NAME OF MODEL - AUTHOR	TOP LEVEL PHASES		TARGET EVIDENCE	
			PHYSICAL	DIGITAL
Scientific Crime Scene Investigation Model (Lee et al. 2001)	1. Recognition 2. Identification	3. Individualization 4. Reconstruction	X	
The Digital Forensic Research Workshop Investigative Model (Palmer, 2001).	1. Identification 2. Preservation 3. Collection	4. Examination 5. Analysis 6. Presentation		X
An Intergraded digital investigation process (Carrier and Spafford, 2003)	1. Readiness Phases 2. Deployment Phases 3. Physical Crime Scene Investigation Phases	4. Digital Crime Scene Investigation Phases 5. Review	X	X
Extended Model of Cybercrime Investigations (Ciardjuain, 2004)	1. Awareness 2. Authorization 3. Planning 4. Notification 5. Search for and identify evidence 6. Collection	7. Transport 8. Storage 9. Examination 10. Hypothesis 11. Presentation 12. Proof / defense 13. Dissemination		X
Computer Forensics Field Triage Process Model (Rogers et al., 2006)	1. Planning 2. Triage 3. User Usage Profile	4. Chronology Timeline 5. Internet 6. Case Specific		X
Systematic Digital Forensic Investigation Model (Agarwal et al., 2011)	1. Preparation 2. Securing the Scene 3. Survey and Recognition 4. Documenting the Scene 5. Communication Shielding	6. Evidence Collection 7. Preservation 8. Examination 9. Analysis 10. Presentation 11. Result		X
Generic Computer Investigation Model (Yusoff et al, 2011)	1. Pre-Process 2. Acquisition and 3. Preservation	4. Analysis 5. Presentation 6. Post-Process	X	X

Table 1: Top level phases of crime investigation models

3. A model for hybrid evidence investigation

The proposed model can be implemented in investigating crime scenes with hybrid evidence, but also in investigations where only digital or only physical evidence exists. The model consists of four major phases and twelve secondary sub-phases (Fig. 1).

3.1 Phase A: Preparation

(A1) Notification. This first step includes: (a) Notification that a crime has been committed. For example using European Emergency Number (112) to report a crime, sending an email, going to a police station etc. (b) Notification to the proper law enforcement agency responsible to conduct the investigation. The responsible agency can be determined by geographical criteria (location of crime scene) or the nature of the crime-incident (robbery, suicide etc.). Notification is very important, because the information collected here is crucial for the next steps of the investigation.

(A2) Authorization. Authorization is obtained from the agency assigned to conduct an investigation. The form and details of the authorization depend on the type of crime and the procedural law of the country where it is committed. Typically, immediately after a crime has been discovered, assigned officers can conduct an investigation at once and inform the attorney on duty as soon as possible.

(A3) Preparation. Preparation includes availability of the necessary tools, equipment and personnel able to conduct the investigation. Preparation is important not only after the notification for a crime or incident but also before, including education and training, response, availability and functionality of tools and equipment. In this sub-phase the person responsible for the investigation is determined.

3.2 Phase B: Crime scene investigation

(B1) Preservation. The Lead first respondent at the crime scene is responsible for organizing a number of things: first aid, search for witnesses and securing the scene from people who are not authorized to approach. Additionally, possible source of physical and digital evidence should also be recognized and secured.

(B2) Identification. This is a specialized task that is preferably conducted by crime investigation experts. Their task is to identify possible evidence, physical or digital related to items set in the crime scene. In serious crimes, the investigation could be conducted by a number of technicians specialized in different fields. Their level of cooperation and understanding is a major factor for a successful investigation. This phase also includes documentation which refers to photographing, sketching and mapping the crime scene, taking notes about items or people present at the crime scene etc.

(B3) Collection – Examination. This is one of the most important sub-phases of the model. The investigator has to collect fingerprints, items related to the crime, biological material and other physical evidence. In case there is digital evidence at the crime scene the investigator should firstly search for volatile data. In this stage the cooperation between the digital and physical crime scene experts is highly important because collection of physical evidence can destroy digital evidence and vice versa. This stage also contains examination. This is not the thorough examination procedure that is conducted in a laboratory environment. However sometimes it is important for the investigation to get as much information as soon as possible. For example in a serious crime investigation it is extremely urgent for the investigator to search the victim's mobile phone for *e.g.*, last calls or messages or a personal computer for e-mails or recent posts on social networks.

(B4) Transportation. Although transportation of evidence is usually perceived as a secondary procedure, we consider it as important as collection. During transportation special measures should be taken to avoid any damage to the evidence. Careful packaging, humidity and temperature, should be considered to avoid any destruction of physical and/or digital evidence.

3.3 Phase C: Laboratory examination

(C1) Examination. The examination of evidence in a laboratory environment is essential to any investigation because it can provide the investigator with crucial evidence related to the case. While at the crime scene only a part of the collected

evidence can be examined, in this phase all evidence is thoroughly examined and analyzed according to the nature of evidence and the specifics of each case.

(C2) Storage. After examination, evidence should be stored properly in a locked evidence room with stringent access controls. The evidence should be labeled and segregated to avoid any cross contamination, to avoid destruction and to enable re-examination if such need occurs in a court or any other step of the investigation.

(C3) Report. The Report determines the outcome of the laboratory examination phase. The report of the lab is one of the most important documents for the investigator and all parties involved in a case (prosecution and defence).

3.4 Phase D: Conclusion

(D1) Reconstruction. Crime reconstruction is the main responsibility of the investigator who evaluates the collected and examined evidence and represents the facts as defined by the evidence analysis. This step is only of value if the previous steps have been followed forensically such that anyone following the same method would arrive at the same results.

(D2) Dissemination. Dissemination is the last step of the model. A thorough review of the investigation is conducted in this step to preserve gained knowledge and identify areas of improvement. Lessons learned should be carefully recorded and disseminated to other parties which conduct similar investigations.

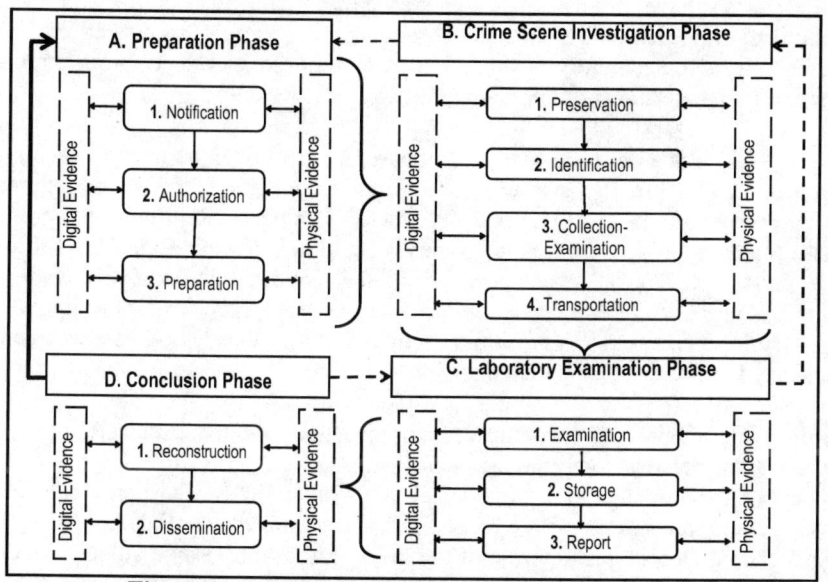

Figure 1: A model for hybrid evidence investigation

4. Model Analysis

The proposed model for hybrid evidence investigation holds the majority of the benefits of the existing models adding an extra advantage: It can be implemented to every crime scene investigation whether digital evidence is present or not. The format of the model resembles a traditional law enforcement investigation model, but it has been adjusted to also face the challenges of digital evidence. The model can be easily interpreted, because it is divided into specified phases and a number of sub-phases. This is very important for the investigators who are called to practice it but also for the trainers who teach crime investigation methods and techniques.

The model examines the whole process of crime investigation, starting from the notification that a crime has been committed, ending to the findings of the research. Digital and physical evidence are equally important and influence every sub-phase of the model (double arrows in Fig. 1). Phase B targets the search and collection of physical and digital evidence, which are in constant interrelation. In this phase, the collection-examination sub-phase is highly important. In the collection sub-phase, there is not a defined order in evidence collection. The investigator is responsible to take a critical decision and determine if volatile and other digital data should have priority over collection of physical evidence such as fingerprints or biological material. The examination sub-phase at the crime scene does not intend to replace the laboratory examination but to help the investigator to collect important evidence crucial for the next steps as soon as the investigation begins. Digital evidence seems to mostly affect this phase; however its role is highly important to all phases of the model. For example, in Phase A, the existence of digital evidence affects the type of authorization needed and the personnel who will conduct the investigation. Unlike previous models, laboratory examination of the collected evidence from the crime scene is a separate and very important phase.

Although there is a defined order in the phases of the model, iteration at each phase or returning to a previous phase is also an option. Inarguably an investigation is a process where a number of unpredictable factors can occur. Returning to a previous phase (marked in Fig. 1 with dotted arrows) could help the investigator to fill in the gaps and ensure that all evidence is adequately collected and analyzed. After the investigation ends, the knowledge gained may be used as feedback to improve the investigation process (straight bold line in Fig. 1) so that lessons learned can be considered in future investigations.

As in every model for law enforcement investigations the responsibility of the investigation belongs to the assigned investigator. He/she is in charge of all the aspects of the investigation, guides experts of other fields who participate in the investigation process and in Phase D he/she draws conclusions about the investigation. Despite the key role of the investigator other people are also involved in the investigation process. For example in Phase A emergency call first responders should collect all the necessary information and report to the proper agency as soon as possible. In Phase B first responders have to secure the crime scene while forensic experts of different fields have to collect and examine primary evidence, possibly of different types, and, finally, in Phase C collected and transported evidence is examined in a laboratory environment by specialized personnel.

5. Conclusions

In this paper, we considered crime scene investigation where digital and physical evidence may co-exist, and presented the key challenges of law enforcement investigation in the new environment. Additionally, we reviewed a selection of investigation models for physical/digital evidence and proposed a model for hybrid evidence investigation. Our model unifies the procedures related to digital and physical evidence collection and examination, taking into consideration the unique characteristics of each form of evidence. Inarguably, the proposed model is still in its infancy. It should be tested and evaluated in real investigation environments and get feedback which would define the necessary modifications. Additionally, a more detailed description of each phase of the model is needed, also supported by a manual for investigators which should include further technical instructions related to an investigation. These are left for future work.

6. References

Agarwal, A., Gupta, M., Gupta, S. and Gupta S.C. (2011), "Systematic Digital Forensic Investigation Model", *International Journal of Computer Science and Security*, Vol. 5, No. 1, pp 118-131.

Beebe, N. (2009), "Digital Forensic Research: The Good, The Bad, and The Unaddressed," in Advances in Digital Forensics V, Peterson G. and Shenoi S. (eds.), Boston, Springer, pp 17-33. ISBN 978-3-642-04154-9.

Carrier, B. and Spafford, E. (2003), "Getting Physical with the Digital Investigation Process, *International Journal of Digital Evidence*, Vol. 2, No. 2.

Ciardhuain, S. (2004), "An Extended Model of Cybercrime Investigations", *International Journal of Digital Evidence*, Vol. 3, No. 1.

Garfinkel, S. (2010), "Digital Forensics Research: The next 10 years", *Digital Investigation*, Vol. 7, pp S64-S73.

Hunton, P. (2010), "Cyber Crime and Security: A New Model of Law Enforcement Investigation", *Policing*, Vol. 4, No. 4, pp. 385-395.

Hunton, P. (2011), "The stages of Cybercrime investigations: Bridging the gap between technology examination and law enforcement investigation", *Computer law and Security Review*, Vol. 27, No. 1, pp. 61-67.

Lee, H., Palmbach, T., and Miller, M. (2001), *Henry Lee's Crime Scene Handbook*, Academic Press, San Diego, ISBN: 0-12-440830-3.

National Institute of Justice (2000), "Crime Scene Investigation, A guide for law enforcement", Research Report, *U.S. Department of Justice*, https://www.ncjrs.gov/pdffiles1/nij/178280.pdf, (Accessed 27 January 2012).

National Institute of Justice (2004), "Forensic Examination of Digital Evidence: A Guide for Law Enforcement", Special Report, U.S. Department of Justice, https://www.ncjrs.gov/pdffiles1/nij/199408.pdf, (Accessed 27 January 2012).

National Institute of Justice (2008), "Electronic Crime Scene Investigation. A Guide for first Respondents", Special Report, Second Edition, U.S. Department of Justice https://www.ncjrs.gov/pdffiles1/nij/219941.pdf, (Accessed 27 January 2012).

Palmer, G. (ed.), (2001), "A Road Map for Digital Forensic Research", Digital Forensic Research Workshop (DFRWS) Technical Report DTR-T001-01, Utica, New York, http://www.dfrws.org/2001/dfrws-rm-final.pdf, (Accessed 27 January 2012).

Palmer, G. (2002), "Forensic Analysis in the Digital World", *International Journal of Digital Evidence*, Vol. 1, No. 1.

Reith, M., Car, C., and Gunsch, G. (2002), "An Examination of Digital Forensic Models", *International Journal of Digital Evidence*, Vol. 1, No. 3.

Rogers M., Goldman J., Mislan R., Wedge T. and Debrota S. (2006), "Computer Forensic Field Triage Process Model", *Journal of Digital Forensics, Security and Law*, Vol. 1, No. 2, pp 19-38.

Sheldon, A. (2005), "The future of forensic computing", *Digital Investigation*, Vol. 2, pp 31-35.

Vlachopoulos, K. (2007). *Electronic Crime*, Nomiki Vivliothiki, Athens, ISBN: 978-960-272-458-3.

Yussof, Y., Ismail, R., and Hassan Z. (2011), "Common Phases of Computer Forensics Investigation Models", *International Journal of Computer Science & Information Technology*, Vol. 3, No. 3, pp 17-31.

Towards Solving the Identity Challenge Faced by Digital Forensics

A. Valjarevic and H. Venter

Department of Computer Science, University of Pretoria
e-mail: alexander@vlatacom.com

Abstract

The importance of digital forensics is on a steady rise. One of the biggest challenges posed to digital forensics is the identity challenge. The authors define the identity challenge as the difficulty to prove beyond reasonable doubt in a court of law that a specific person was using a specific identity of a digital subject at a certain time. In order to meet or at least decrease this challenge, organised action within the digital forensics field is needed. The authors propose a set of requirements to be introduced within digital forensics in order to help solve this issue. These requirements include the following: defining the principles of digital identity within digital forensics; introducing strong authentication methods for all information systems and electronic devices; introducing digital signatures for all transactions within information systems and electronic devices; constant interaction with other relevant fields and last but not least, putting an end to internet anonymity. The authors believe that, if implemented, the proposed requirements would not only bring about the higher admissibility of digital evidence related to digital identity in a court of law, but also increase the efficiency of digital forensic investigations.

Keywords

Identity, Digital Identity, Identity Challenge, Digital Forensics, Information Security

1. Introduction

Information technology is advancing at a high rate and modern society is becoming more dependant on it. Together with the increase of incidents requiring digital forensic investigations, this makes digital forensics rapidly gaining in importance. One of the aims of the digital forensic process is to produce (through a process of digital evidence analysis) a hypothesis on who did what, where and how, regarding the incident being investigated. The question of *who* is crucial, especially if the digital forensic process were to lead to the presentation of findings in a court of law. Digital forensic investigators have to link identity of a digital subject (hereafter referred to as a 'digital identity') to a human identity. This is a challenging task.

It is against this background that the authors have defined the following problem statement. The problem is that the identity challenge faced by digital forensic investigations is increasing. We define the concept "identity challenge" as the effort to prove beyond reasonable doubt in a court of law that a specific human has used a specific identity of a digital subject at a certain time. Lack of awareness of this challenge might become a great obstacle in the development of digital forensics as a whole. There is a need to define requirements that have to be obliged by digital forensics scientists and practitioners in order to make progress towards solving this challenge.

The first section of this paper has introduced the paper and the problem statement. Section 2 gives background on digital forensics, attribution, digital identity and legal requirements. The following section proposes requirements for solving the identity challenge faced by digital forensics. Section 4 discusses the proposed requirements, their benefits and associated challenges. The last section concludes the paper and indicates possible future research work.

2. Background

An overview of digital forensics, attribution, digital identity and legal requirements regarding digital evidence is provided in the following subsections.

2.1. On Digital Forensics

In this section the authors wish to explain the basic principles and importance of digital forensics.

Digital Forensics is defined as the use of scientifically derived and proven methods toward the preservation, collection, validation, identification, analysis, interpretation, documentation and presentation of digital evidence derived from digital sources for the purpose of facilitating or furthering the reconstruction of events found to be criminal, or helping to anticipate unauthorised actions shown to be disruptive to planned operations (Palmer, 2001). The digital forensic process comprises several phases. The authors define these phases as: Incident detection, First response, Planning, Preparation, Incident scene documentation, Potential evidence identification, Potential evidence collection, Potential evidence transportation, Potenial evidence storage, Potential evidence analysis, Presentation and Conclusion. (Other authors define phases differently and there is currently no consensus for a single process model in the digital forensics community.) Analysis of the potential digital evidence is performed in order to make a hypothesis on how the incident occurred, what its exact characteristics are and who is to be held responsible. In this paper, we concentrate on proposeing requirements to digital forenics that could make it easier to identify the person to be held responsible for a particular incident.

The importance of the digital forensics can be seen through the fact that, by the time of writing, we have an entire forensic community. For example, there exists a digital forensics group on Linkedin, called the Digital Forensic Association, which has over 4000 members. The importance of digital forensics can be also seen in the light of the large number of national and international bodies that are working towards the development and standardisation of this discipline. (i.e. The European Network of Forensic Science Institutes, The International Organization on Computer Evidence, International Federation for Information Processing Work Group 11.9 on Digital

Forensics etc.) There are also numerous evidence units and laboratories that are well funded and that produce forensically sound digital evidence.

2.2. On attribution

This section gives an overview of attribution in the light of digital forensics.

Attribution is defined as determining the identity or location of an attacker or an attacker's intermediary (Wheeler and Larsen, 2003). In (Hunker et al., 2008) it is stated that sufficient attribution may be satisfied by knowing the IP address of the host that initiated the attack, identifying the originator's e-mail address, locating the physical location of the source of the attack or by identifying the actual individual who was at the attacking computer. In this paper, however, we are concentrating only on the issue of identifying the actual individual who was responsible for a certain action in digital realm. To achieve successful attribution, investigators today have to introduce methods and techniques outside of the digital forensics and cooperate with investigators performing the physical investigation. Techniques used include authorship attribution (i.e. through typing pattern biometrics, stylometry), introducing circumstantial evidence from physical forensics investigations (i.e. the suspect was in the room where computer, used for committing cyber-crime, is located, based on interviews with witnesses). Ideally, a digital forensics investigation would be able to produce direct and circumstantial evidence sufficient for the successful identification of the individual involved in the incident being investigated.

The next section explains the basics of digital identity.

2.3. On Digital Identity

Digital identity can be defined as the digital representation of a set of claims made by one digital subject about itself or another digital subject (Cameron, 2006). Note that this paper concentrates solely on digital identity associated to humans. Also note that a human can not have a digital identity, for the simple fact that a human cannot exist in the digital realm. However, a human can use a certain digital identity and be responsible for that use. In order to make the above clearer we provide some definitions of some terms used so far.

"A *digital subject* can be defined as a representation of a person, or a representation or existence of a thing in the digital realm, that is being described or dealt with." This definition was constructed by modifying the definition in (Cameron, 2006). Examples of digital subjects would be a user account belonging to a human, an avatar in a computer game, an IP address of a computer, digital resources (e.g. files) operating system, etc. Further, if we concentrate on the digital identity of humans, we can say: "A *digital subject* is a representation of a person in the digital realm."

"*The claim* is defined as an assertion of the truth of something, typically one that is disputed or in doubt (Cameron, 2006)." Examples of claims made about a digital subject would be that the user account has a certain password, or that the IP address of a computer has a certain digital certificate associated to it, etc.

Thus, a typical example of a digital identity would be the claim that a certain user account on a certain operating system has a certain username and password. Further, let us try to define how human identity can be connected to digital identity.

The process of verifying the validity of a claimed identity (human identity) is known as authentication. Thus, the identity of a person can be confirmed only through appropriate authentication. Different forms of the authentication for human identity exist, including (Stewart et al., 2008): PIN numbers, passwords, favourite colour, etc. (*something you know* type of credentials); One-time pads, usb drives, smart-cards, digital certificates, state issued documents (*something you have* type of credentials); Biometrics– fingerprints, iris pattern, vane pattern, hand geometry, voice, face geometry, keystroke pattern (*something you are* type of credentials). In modern information systems it is considered good practice to introduce multi-level authentication (Stewart et al., 2008), where different types of authentication credentials are used in combination with one another, e.g. providing a password together with using a biometric trait such as a fingerprint.

In (Milgate, 2006) identity is defined as a relationship between one entity and a particular registration. The authors would rephrase this to the following: "The connection between the identity of a human and a digital identity is established through registration." An example would be a person registering an email account. We can only claim that a certain human used a certain digital identity when the identity authentication process was performed during registration and/or before each particular use of the digital identity. Figure 1 illustrates the concept of digital identity and the connection between human identity and digital identity. Namely, digital identity is formed with set of claims and digital subject and then is connected to human identity through process of registration, which should include identity authentication. Human identity exists solely in physical realm. Digital identity exists solely in digital realm.

The next section provides an overview of legal requirements regarding digital evidence and digital identity.

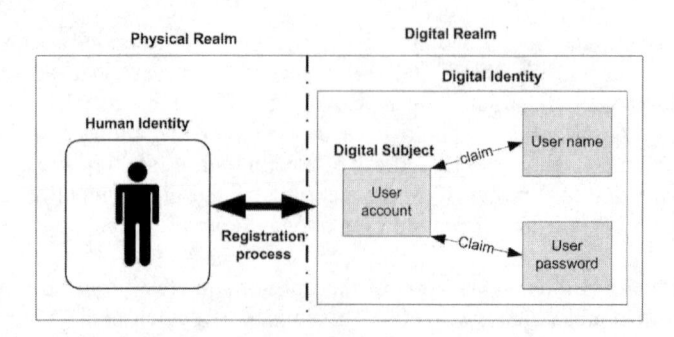

Figure 1: Concept of digital identity and connection with human identity

2.4. Legal requirements

In this section the authors give an overview of the legal requirements pertaining to digital forensics and especially the admissibility of digital evidence in a court of law. It should be noted that legal requirements may differ extensively in different jurisdictions across the world. The premise of this section is not to advocate specific legal systems, but rather to note the generic requirements in terms of legal issues that should be adopted by the legal system of a specific jurisdiction.

For example, in the United Stated of America cases that include the presentation of digital evidence are treated under rule 702 of the Federal Rules of Evidence. For application of this rule, the Daubert case (Daubert v. Merrell Dow Pharmaceuticals, 1993) is the most important. In the Daubert case, the court suggested the following factors to be considered: whether the theories and techniques employed by the scientific expert have been tested; whether they have been subjected to peer review and publication; whether the techniques employed by the expert have a known error rate; whether they are subject to standards governing their application; and whether the theories and techniques employed by the expert enjoy widespread acceptance. Other countries have similar requirements regarding the admissibility of digital evidence.

It is notable however that there are no established legal requirements for accepting the claim that certain digital identity has been used by certain person at certain time. Proving that certain digital identity has been used by certain person at certain time can be challenging. Following case clearly depicts that challenge (Leyden, 2003). Aaron Caffrey was arrested under the suspicion of launching a denial of service attack against the Port of Houston's systems. The defense claimed that Trojan was installed on the defendant's computer and that attack was performed by the Trojan. The digital forensics investigation showed no sign of a Trojan, and did find tools used for attack on the computer, but could not rule out that a Trojan may have been in volatile storage media. The jury unanimously decided that the defendant was not guilty.

The next section explains the proposed requirements to be imposed in order to solve the identity challenge faced by digital forensics.

3. Requirements for solving the identity challenge

The authors propose the following requirements to be imposed on digital forensics in order to decrease the impact of the identity challenge: Definition of the principles of digital identity within digital forensics science, Introduction of multi-level authentication for all digital devices and information system, Introduction of digital signing of all digital transactions where possible, Interaction with fields of digital identity, identity management and biometrics, Terminating anonymity on Internet.

The subsections that follow discuss each of the above requirements in more detail.

3.1. Requirement 1 (Principles requirement): Definition of principles of digital identity within digital forensics science

The authors believe that it is essential for digital identity and digital identity principles to be defined within the science of digital forensics. Not only must digital identity itself be defined, but the principles have to be defined of how a specific digital identity can be associated with a specific person. These principles could later be used in a court of law in order to achieve higher admisibility of digital evidence. These definitions must be comprehensive and have to take into account as many as possible different types of information systems and electronic devices.

The main challenge for implementation of this requirement would be to achieve consensus in the digital forensics community and to enforce the use of the principles in a court of law, through cooperation with legal authorities. However, the authors firmly believe that achieving this requirement is possible and highly needed.

3.2. Requirement 2 (Authentication requirement): Introduction of multi-level authentication for all digital devices and information systems

The authors believe that there should be a requirement that the verification of identity – when accessing or registering to use a digital device or an information system (at all levels, i.e. OS, application and firmware) – should be performed via multi-factor authentication, for example requiring biometrics, a digital certificate and a password. There should be an interface to an identity management system within every electronic device and information system. (Such identity management system can be embedded within the device, or it can work as a standalone and be independent from other devices or information systems.) The interface with the identity management system should ensure that proper management of identities is performed. One physical person should have one identity (not limited to one role) within the device or system.

The authors understand that the implementation of this requirement would be challenging in terms of needed expenditure, technology development, and technology accessibility to users. We, however, do believe that in years to come the expenditure needed would become lower and technology needed for implementation would become more accessible.

3.3. Requirement 3 (Digital signatures): Introduction of digital signing of all digital transactions where possible

The authors believe that all transactions performed within any digital device or information system should be digitally signed by the entity performing the transaction. Note that we use the term *entity*. An entity can be any digital subject. This would enable non-repudiation and accountability for all transactions and would therefore decrease the identity challenge faced by digital forensics. It would also permit more efficient digital investigations due to the fact that transactions would be more easily tracked.

Digital signatures are now accepted all over the world as valid for authorising transactions. Within the European Union, for example, the Electronic Signature Directive (Directive 1999/93/EC, 2000) defines an electronic signature and what the legal effects of electronic signatures are. Similar statements are made in the South African Electronic Communications and Transactions Act (Electronic Communications and Transactions Act, South Africa, 2002). It is clear from this that appropriate legislature exists and supports the introduction of digital signatures for electronic (digital) transactions.

The challenges anticipated are as same as for *Requirement 3*. The authors believe that the implementation of this requirement (*Requirement 4*) would become possible in terms of needed expenditure and technology in the foreseeable future.

3.4. Requirement 4 (Interaction requirement): Interaction with fields of digital identity, identity management and biometrics

It is vital that digital forensic scientists and practitioners should constantly cooperate and interact with scientists and practitioners from the fields of digital identity, identity management and biometrics. Such collaboration is not limited to these fields and includes other fields that might have an interest in digital identity or digital forensics. Digital forensics has to take into account all the latest discoveries and practical solutions in these fields so as to stay up to date and geared up to adjust and improve in line with changes in these fields. Interaction would be facilitated most successfully through the introduction of common international bodies consisting of scientists and practitioners from all relevant fields.

3.5. Requirement 5 (No anonymity on the Internet): Terminating anonymity on the Internet

First of all, the authors want to stress that they believe that terminating anonymity on the Internet does not and should not mean putting an end to privacy on the Internet. The authors believe that if appropriate mechanisms and policies are in place, privacy on the Internet does not require anonymity. Future technological solutions should enforce the verification of digital identity when accessing or using information systems, while protecting personal identifiable information of the users.

It is striking to note that, most often, no identity authentication is performed when a person registers to use a certain digital subject (i.e. email account) on the Internet. This enables anonymity and privacy on the Internet, but makes the work of digital forensic investigators much harder. For example, hacker groups such as Anonymous and LulzSec have their own websites and social network accounts (i.e. twitter.com/lulzsec, http://lulzsecurity.com). Even though the digital identities are known, these cannot easily be linked with the identities of the human beings.

The authors believe that in order for every individual to be accountable for his/her actions on the Internet, it essential that no anonymity exists. This would enable digital forensic practitioners to associate digital identities on the Internet with the physical identities in a quick and easy manner. Many calls have been heard for abandoning this custom of anonymity, but serious concerns about privacy remain a major reason for the inaction in this regard. The authors believe that the global society must take responsibility for the Internet and initiate action while implementing all that should still ensure the preservation of Internet users' privacy. The authors understand very well that implementing a measure such as terminating anonymity on the Internet would require world-wide discussions that would have to involve stakeholders and participants from all the relevant fields, ranging from law to information technology and from national security agencies to civil society representatives. We do recognize that this action would be against current legal environments in some countries, i.e. in The United States of America, but we expect that these legal environments could be changed if broader consensus is reached on this matter. The authors also realise that implementing this requirement would come at a cost and entail significant investments in hardware and software infrastructure of the Internet. They nevertheless believe that this requirement is essential from a digital forensics point of view, and are confident that abandoning anonymity on the Internet would hold much benefit in the long term.

Finally, note the following. In Facebook's Statement of Rights and Responsibilities, it is said: "Facebook users provide their real names and information... You will not provide any false personal information on Facebook, or create an account for anyone other than yourself without permission..." In Google's Terms of service, it is said: "...you may be required to provide information about yourself (such as identification or contact details) as part of the registration process for the service, or as part of your continued use of the services. You agree that any registration information you give to Google will always be accurate, correct and up to date." The above-mentioned examples practically mean that there are numerous service providers on the internet who do require personally identifiable information when you register to use the services, and still the bulk of the people using these services have no objection on that. But, how can a service provider guarantee that the supplied information is accurate? Currently it is very hard, and that is why it is now possible and common practice that people register user accounts by supplying other people's or imaginary personally identifiable information. Therefore, mechanisms should be in place to ensure identity authentication when registering to use services on the Internet, which would ensure the users conform to terms of service that they have accepted.

Of all the requirements proposed, this one is the most challenging. The implementation of this requirement would entail significant expenditure into developing and implementing technological solutions needed to end anonymity on internet, while preserving privacy of the users. A significant challenge would also be the development or change of existing legislature to accomodate for this requirement, or to implement the requirement in such a way that would not contravene current legislature. The agreement of the global community would be needed, which might be extremely hard to achieve. Inspite of all the challenges, the authors believe that the time for implementation of this requirement would be possible in the foreseeable future, due to technological advancements and the increasing importance of digital forensics.

4. Discussion

In this paper, the authors give a comprehensive explanation of digital identity and how it can be connected to a human identity, and propose a set of requirements to decrease the identity challenge faced by digital forensics. The proposed requirements are high-level statements and should be further developed by the entire digital forensics community. Note that the implementation guidelines, methods and techniques are outside the scope of this document. If implemented, these requirements can bring about multiple benefits for digital forensics, such as the higher admissibility of digital evidence pertaining to digital identity in a court of law, and preventing the identity challenge from becoming even more problematic. In addition, the implementation of these requirements might make digital investigations into digital identity issues more efficient and effective, both in regards of identifying humans involved.

It should be stressed that in order to implement these requirements, the engagement of the digital forensics community at large will be needed. An implementation plan needs to be developed in accordance with legal requirements and current technology capabilities. The work must be performed in close cooperation with other relevant fields such as identity management, biometrics and public key infrastructure in order for the implementation plan to be in line with current trends and technologies in these fields. For example, it should be taken into account that what we consider a suitable means of verifying identity today might not be suitable tomorrow. For example, we can envisage that with the development of more powerful computers with high processing power, public key infrastructure with current key lengths may become obsolete. Further, consensus on the requirements is needed in the digital forensics community if implementation is to be effective. The authors believe that the proposed requirements should bring about significant changes. Support from national and international bodies that govern information technology development, Internet and information security would be needed, together with support from the governments themselves in order for all or some of the requirements to be accepted and implemented. The authors also realise that the proposed requirements imply that significant expenditure has to be incurred. Technological advancement and cost efficiency of the solutions for implementing these requirements would teherfore play a major role in acceptance of the requirements.

5. Conclusion

Let us revisit the problem statement. The problem is that the identity challenge faced by digital forensics is increasing. Thus, it is currently difficult for digital forensic scientists and investigators to prove beyond reasonable doubt in a court of law that a specific human being used a specific identity of a digital subject at a certain time. In an attempt to address this problem, the authors proposed a set of requirements to be imposed for the sake of digital forensics. These requirements constitute a first step towards solving the identity challenge. The authors strongly believe that, if implemented, these requirements will have multiple benefits, among others enhancing the admissibility of digital evidence related to a digital identity in a court of law and improving efficiency of digital investigations.

We also realise that such requirements cannot suddenly all happen over night; it will take time. The person reading this might also perceive these requirements as a Utopia. Feel not alone, since the authors also realise that some of these requirements are far fetched. However, if one thinks with an open mind about the huge advantages some of these requirements are posing, then surely they cannot simply be ignored. It is not impossible to accomplish such requirements, albeit, it will be a mammoth task. The authors hope, however, that this paper will lay a corner stone towards the prospect of solving the identity challenge in the digital realm.

Future research work in this regard will include defining lower-level requirements and proposing an implementation plan. This will have to be done systematically with the aid of the entire digital forensic community and with support from the wider information security research community and other interested parties.

6. References

Cameron, K. (2006), "Laws of Identity", http://www.identityblog.com/?p=352, (Accessed 01.02.2012)

Daubert v. Merrell Dow Pharmaceuticals Inc. (1993), 509 U.S. 579

Directive 1999/93/EC of the European Parliament and of the Council of 13 December 1999 on a Community framework for electronic signatures, O.J. L 13/12, 19 January 2000 (2000)

Electronic Communications and Transactions Act, Act No. 25 of 2002, Republic of South Africa (2002)

Hunker, J., Hutchinson, B., Margulies, J. (2008), "Role and Challenges for Sufficient Cyber-Attack Attribution", Institute for Information Infrastructure Protection

Leyden, J. (2003), "Caffrey acquittal a setback for cybercrime prosecution", The Register U.K. Press 3

Milgate, A. (2006), "The Identity Dictionary", http://identityaccessman.blogspot.com, (Accessed 01.02.2012)

Palmer, G. (2001), "A Road Map for Digital Forensic Research", *Technical Report DTR-T001-01*, Report from the First Digital Forensic Research Workshop (DFRWS)

Pollitt, M.M. (2001), "Report on digital evidence", 13th Interpol Forensic Science Symposium, Lyon, France

Stewart, J.M., Tittel, E., Chapple, M. (2008), "*Certified Information Systems Security Professional Study Guide*", Fourth Edition, Wiley Publishing, Inc., Indianapolis, Indiana, ISBN: 978-0-470-27688-4.

Wheeler, D.A. and Larsen, G.N. (2003), "Techniques for Cyber Attack Attribution", *IDA Paper*, Institute for Defense Analysis, P-3792.

Arguments and Methods for Database Data Model Forensics

H. Q. Beyers[1], M.S. Olivier[2] and G.P. Hancke[1]

[1]Department of Electrical, Electronic and Computer Engineering,
University of Pretoria, Pretoria, South Africa
[2]Department of Computer Science, University of Pretoria, Pretoria, South Africa
e-mail: hqbeyers@gmail.com

Abstract

A Database Management System (DBMS) consists of metadata and data. The metadata influences the way the data is presented to the user and this presents various forensic complications. The data model can be viewed as the highest level of metadata which governs the way other metadata and data in the DBMS are presented to the user. The data model can be modified to hide or tamper with forensic evidence. In this study the focus is on the data model of the DBMS and arguments are provided to indicate why the data model is an important consideration when conducting a forensic investigation on a DBMS. Various methods are presented to transform the data model into a desired state for a forensic investigation and these methods are measured against set out criteria. No one method is adequate for every forensic investigation. A forensic investigator should understand the various methods and select the correct data model state and method to convert the data model into that required state.

Keywords

Database Forensics, Data Model, Database Layers

1 Introduction

A Database Management System (DBMS) consists of various layers which can either be a form of metadata or data (Dyche, 2000). The ANSI-SPARC Architecture divided the database into various layers (ANSI/X3/SPARC Study Group, 1975). Some layers in the DBMS may influence the actions and results of other abstract layers and this fact presents a variety of vulnerabilities and forensic possibilities (Olivier, 2009). Based on the ANSI-SPARC Architecture, we divided the metadata and data of the DBMS into four abstract layers and assembled the metadata in order to get different results from the DBMS (Beyers et al. 2011). The first abstract layer of the DBMS is the data model which is a type of metadata and can be viewed as the source code of the DBMS. The second layer of the DBMS is the data dictionary which can be viewed as metadata that gets utilised to construct all the databases of the DBMS. The application schema includes user created operations that can manipulate data such as database triggers, procedures, and sequences, as well as the logical grouping of database objects such as views and tables. The fourth abstract layer is the application data which is the rows stored within the tables of a DBMS.

In this study the focus will fall on the data model abstract layer (source code) of the DBMS, because it can be viewed as the highest level of metadata which influences other metadata and data in the DBMS. The data model of a DBMS interprets the metadata and data stored in the DBMS and delivers the results accordingly, but the data model is code which can be altered to deliver almost any result. The data model can be changed to tamper with evidence such as table structures, records in a table etc. (Beyers *et al.* 2011). Similar to any other software program, the source code of the DBMS may present some flaws and vulnerabilities (Litchfield, 2005).

Our premise is that the ideal tool to examine the contents of a database will often be a DBMS: it provides powerful query facilities that enable the investigator to express the wish to easily formulate exactly what data is of interest. Possibilities exist to correlate sets of data, or to find data that is inconsistent with other data. Possibilities exist to formulate simple queries just like a typical user would have done it. Possibilities exist to query the metadata to determine the structure of data. And so on. However, in order to use the DBMS as a tool for such forensic database examination we need to know that we can rely on it to provide forensically useful results. Formulated slightly differently, the challenge is to combine the data to be investigated with a DBMS that is deemed reliable enough. Note that *reliable enough*, in general, means that the tool being used should exhibit sufficiently low error rates. The phrases *sufficiently low* or *reliable enough* are, amongst others, influenced by whether the case at hand is a criminal or civil matter, and whether the outcomes are to be used for evidentiary purposes or some lesser role in an investigation. This paper examines various ways in which a DBMS may be combined with data to be examined. It assumes the data to be examined is located on some computer that potentially contains evidence. For such data to be examined only two alternatives exist: either the data is examined on the computer where it is located, or the data is somehow imaged and copied to a forensic machine. This paper works systematically through the viable options, examines how the option may be effected in an examination and determines the reliability of such an option in qualitative terms.

These viable options will transform the data model into a required state. The state of the data model will have to fulfil one or more of the following criteria.

- Provide an environment where the evidence output from the DBMS is trustworthy and have not been altered by the data model.
- Provide an environment where the processes used to acquire consistent evidence from the DBMS have not altered the evidence.

In order to discuss the various methods and whether their outcomes adhere to the criteria mentioned above, this study is structured into the following four key areas. The various reasons why either a found data model or clean data model is important are discussed. In the next section a range of methods are presented to achieve a clean or found data model environment. The following section explains how this study fits into the bigger picture of database management system forensics and the remaining three abstract layers. Finally, a conclusion is presented.

2   Forensic Environment with a Clean or Found Data Model

The previous section briefly discussed how the data model may influence the output of the DBMS. Two types of data model forensic environments will now be explored; the clean and found environment. The difference between these two environments is that the found environment contains the original data model that was present when the incident of forensic interest occurred, while the clean environment represents an environment where the data model has been cleaned up in such a way that we can trust the data model. The found environment can further be divided into a found environment that either resides on the live machine or a found environment that is copied onto a completely different machine. In this section the various reasons why the found or the clean environments are useful will be discussed. Several scenarios are presented where the found or clean environments are advantageous.

2.1   Arguments for a Clean Data Model Environment

The clean environment is a setting where we have ensured that the data model will not alter the output of the DBMS. It is important to understand that a clean state differs from a post-mortem state characteristic of traditional digital forensics. A clean state is not merely a copy of the evidence that needs to be analysed, but rather a copy of the evidence program that runs like the original copy and from which we can query output. This means that the clean environment is set up to run like the original DBMS, but we are sure that the data model is not corrupting the output that we receive from the DBMS. The various reasons why it can be important consist of the following: (1) the data model as code, (2) the data model as a rootkit, and (3) the data model as a toolkit.

1. The Data Model as Code
The data model is the underlying software that controls the way the metadata and data of the DBMS are utilised. Just like any other code, the data model might have the ability and authority to control the way the metadata and data of the DBMS is stored, interpreted and processed. We can imagine that the code can be changed in endless different ways to achieve almost any outcome. Depending on the DBMS, the source code may be freely available on the internet. An attacker can edit the code to execute the attacker's intended commands before installing or updating the compromised code on a host or server. Due to the fact that the data model can be rewritten to execute malicious tasks, hide data etc. it is important to ensure that the data model is clean when doing a forensic analysis.

2. The Data Model Rootkit
In this section we discuss the second reason why a clean data model state could be required. Rootkits may replace programs or executable files on a host to execute a different task than the executable file was originally intended to execute (Jakobsson and Ramzan, 2008). Rootkits are well known to attack operating systems, but it is possible that a rootkit may attack a DBMS. The database is similar to an operating system because both have users, processes and executables. Red Database Security (Kornbrust, 2005) illustrated how the Oracle database can be attacked by a rootkit.

Users were hidden in the database by inserting a username in the users table and then rewriting rules of a view to not display the inserted username. The view name in Oracle was sys.all_users and was changed to system.all_users and was set up to refer to the original view, but concealing some users. In a similar fashion the database processes were hidden by changing the view name of where the processes are stored from vsession to v_session.

An intruder can install a rootkit on a DBMS by acquiring access to the database through default password guessing, TNS Listener Exploits, Operating System Exploits etc. The example of installing a rootkit in an Oracle database is illustrated by Kornbrust (2005). (1) Create a file rootkit.sql on your own webserver. (2) Insert a HTTP-call into the glogin.sql file on the attacked DBMS client. (3) The next time the database administrator logs into the attacked DBMS the rootkit.sql is downloaded from the webserver. Then the rootkit.sql file is executed to disable terminal output, create a user, modify data dictionary objects, download and execute a keylogger (keylogger.exe), or do any other malicious task. A clean installation of the data model is required to ensure that the forensic evidence collection process will not be influenced by a rootkit.

3. Data Model as a Toolkit
Lastly we have a look at how the DBMS and its data model can be used as a toolkit. This is the third reason why a clean data model state could be required. Toolkits need to ensure that the evidence collection process does not alter the evidence at the same time. The EnCase toolkit brought about a revolution in the digital forensic arena when it introduced the concept of a toolkit that mounts the bit-stream forensic images as read-only virtual devices, therefore disabling any alteration of evidence on the digital device (Casey, 2010). We argue that the data model of the DBMS can also be considered as a type of digital forensic toolkit to extract evidence from the DBMS. While an operating system forensic toolkit extracts registry entries, retrieves deleted data, or validates partitions from the operating system, the data model acts as a forensic toolkit by providing records in tables, logging information and reporting database structures. Therefore it is important that the data model is in a state where the output it delivers can be trusted.

If the data model is used as a digital forensic toolkit, it should adhere to the requirements of a digital forensic toolkit. A toolkit should be (Daniel, 2012): (1) Definable. You must be able to state the problem, describe the desired outcome, develop the algorithm and validate the process. (2) Predictable. The tool must be designed to function in a predictable manner across any usage of the tool. (3) Repeatable. The function must be repeatable within a small error range. (4) Verifiable. The output must be able to be verified in various toolkit testing environments. When we have a clean data model we can say that the data model will be definable, predictable and repeatable. We argue that the data model can be used as a digital forensic toolkit when the data model is clean.

2.2 Arguments for a Found Data Model Environment

A found environment refers to a state of the data model where the data model was in use in the DBMS when an event of forensic interest occurred. The found environment may also refer to an environment where the same machine where the DBMS was originally installed is not used, but the data model was mirrored onto another machine. It is vital to understand that the found environment is not exactly the same here as the traditional meaning of a live digital forensic environment, due to the fact that the environment may fully or partially exist on the live machine or on another machine. In this section reasons are discussed why there might be a need for a found data model environment when conducting a DBMS forensic investigation consisting of: (1) cost of forensic investigation, (2) testing a hypothesis, and (3) simple queries.

1. Cost of Forensic Investigation
A vital consideration before conducting a forensic investigation is to determine how great the cost of the forensic investigation will be. Each technique of conducting a forensic investigation has a different level of complexity and different resource cost (R. Overill *et al.* 2009). These resource costs include the hiring of the expertise to conduct the investigation, the time that the investigation might take and the tools that the experts require to complete the investigation. A found investigation can be a very cost-effective investigation where the forensic investigator can log into the database and use simple database queries to extract all the evidence that is required. The first reason why an investigation of a DBMS with a found data model can be useful is due to its lower cost.

2. Testing a Hypothesis
The second reason why a found data model might be useful for a forensic investigation is to test a hypothesis. A hypothesis is an informed supposition to explain the observations in the data gathering phase of a forensic investigation (Casey, 2010). In other words, a hypothesis is a theory which an investigator might have about what occurred and this theory needs to be tested. A hypothesis might need to be tested in the DBMS, but there is no need to change the data model environment in order to test the hypothesis. In fact it is better to test a hypothesis when we know that the data model and underlying code is in the same state when the event of forensic interest occurred. In this instance a found data model will be useful to test the hypothesis.

3. Simple Queries
The third reason why a found data model can be useful during a forensic investigation is to run simple queries that will have no noticeable effect on the operations or state of the DBMS. The results that the found data model gives as output can still not be trusted entirely, but in some cases it might not be that critical to replace or cleanse all the code of the data model. There may be a situation where the investigator needs to search for clues and not forensic evidence. In this case the database may not be the primary suspect in the investigation, but rather an

independent witness. Only a found data model can provide the forensic investigators with such quick access to data.

3 How to Achieve Various States of the Data Model

Thus far this study has discussed why there is a need to do a forensic investigation on either a clean or found data model environment. In this section we will discuss various methods on how to achieve a clean or found data model state. The practical details in this section were limited due to document length constraints, but will be released in future work.

3.1 Clean Environment

To transform a data model into a clean state requires that the data model is transformed into a condition where the forensic investigator can trust the data model and be certain that the output of the DBMS is in no way corrupted by the data model. In short the data needs to remain the same, but the source code needs to be replaced or cleansed. A critical requirement for the transformation of the data model to a clean state is that the process is forensically sound and does not corrupt the data model even further. Various methods to achieve a clean data model are discussed in this section consisting of: (1) copying data files, (2) recovering the DBMS, and (3) patching the DBMS.

1. Copying Files
One of the approaches to achieve a clean state of the data model is to copy the data files from the suspect installation of the DBMS to a new installation of the DBMS, where a clean copy of the DBMS has been installed. The logic here is that a new installation of the DBMS on another machine will provide a clean data model. The data files of the new installation will be replaced with the data files of the suspect installation. A clean data model along with the data that exist on the suspect machine will then be achieved. This process has been tested with positive results on a PostgreSQL DBMS in one of our studies (Beyers *et al*. 2011). This copy process is illustrated in figure 1. This method adheres to both data model criteria. The data model will not alter the evidence and the evidence can be trusted.

Suspect Installation — New Installation

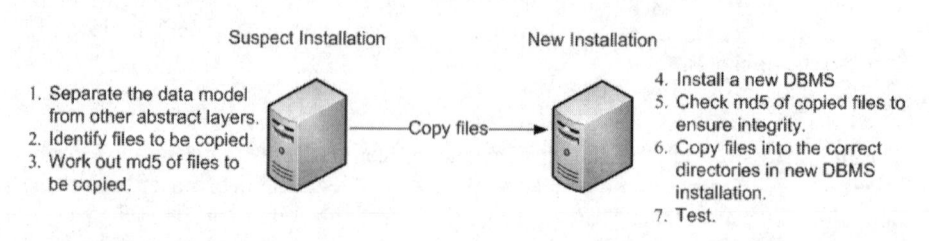

1. Separate the data model from other abstract layers.
2. Identify files to be copied.
3. Work out md5 of files to be copied.

—Copy files—

4. Install a new DBMS
5. Check md5 of copied files to ensure integrity.
6. Copy files into the correct directories in new DBMS installation.
7. Test.

Figure 1: The copy process to achieve a clean data model is displayed.

2. Recover DBMS

Another approach to achieve a clean data model state in the DBMS is to recover the DBMS to a previous state with backup data. If we have adequate backup data of the DBMS we can recover the DBMS to a state that is similar to the state of the suspect DBMS, but with a clean data model. Old data dumps of the entire DBMS will work particularly well in this instance because data dumps will include the application schema and application data if the data dump was made before the DBMS was corrupted. Another source of recovery data is a backup server for the DBMS where it can be proven that the backup server was not compromised and we can trust the data model (Curtis Preston, 2007).

Once we have the acceptable amount of backup data we need to install a clean copy of the DBMS onto another machine. The installation should be exactly the same as the suspect DBMS and all patches and add-ons should be updated and installed. The application data and application schema can then be imported to the new DBMS installation by either entering the data through the DBMS console interface or by making use of the DBMS's data import tools. Unlike the Copying Files method, this method makes use of the clean data model to import the data into the clean DBMS installation. If the investigation requires that the data must be as similar as possible to the suspect DBMS's data it might be useful to run any scripts on the data that would have run on the suspect machine. This is a practical approach to accomplish a clean data model, because it is common practice to make regular backups of the DBMS either to a FTP server or a backup server with a DBMS installed on it. This method adheres to at least one of the two criteria because the data model can be trusted, and if the out-dated backup data has no effect on the evidence, this method will also not alter the evidence of the DBMS.

3. Patching the DBMS

Another method to achieve a clean data model is by patching the DBMS. A DBMS patch is software designed to fix problems or update the software of the DBMS (Greenwald *et al.* 2011). A patch has the potential to update the data model of the DBMS and thus provides a clean and trusted (or at least a partially trusted) data model by merely running a patch script. The patch is a trusted source of code and if this code can replace the untrusted data model code a clean or cleaner data model may be achieved effortlessly. The two scenarios when this method can be utilised is: to clean up the entire data model to acquire trusted results, or to fix odd results that are retrieved on the suspect DBMS by cleansing the data model with a patch. In the first scenario it needs to be determined if there is a patch for the relevant DBMS that will clean up the entire data model without influencing the evidence within the DBMS. Patches will specify precisely what parts of the DBMS the patch will update in the patch readme and the extent of the data model clean-up can be determined from the specification. In the second scenario the suspect DBMS gives unexpected output that could be caused by various reasons such as hidden data, malicious code, etc. A patch may be applied to attempt to eliminate the incorrect output and reveal new evidence. If changes occurred between the suspect DBMS's output and patched DBMS's output, the patch readme document will provide us with a focus area to determine where in the data model the problem occurred.

The DBMS must be installed on another machine with the same DBMS version and add-ons as the suspect DBMS to make sure the installation creates all required configuration on the new machine. Then the files of the entire original DBMS needs to be copied onto the new machine. The hash must be calculated to ensure that no data has changed in the copy process from the original machine to the new machine. The copied files of the original DBMS must now replace the files in the new installation. Finally the selected patches should be applied to the new DBMS installation. The new DBMS copy can now be tested and the investigation can start on the clean DBMS. An advantage of this method is that we can find an almost exact copy of the suspect DBMS, because we do not have to revert to a backup. A disadvantage of this method is the fact that it might be difficult to prove that the patch will clean up the entire data model. This method adheres to both the criteria. The data model can be trusted and the evidence will not be altered.

3.2 Found Environment

The previous section discussed the various methods that can be used to achieve a clean state of the data model which will be acceptable for a forensic investigation. In this section the discussion will include methods to achieve a found data model environment which is acceptable to conduct a forensic investigation in. A found data model involves that the original data model of the DBMS is utilised to conduct a forensic investigation. The various methods to conduct an investigation on a found data model consist of: (1) an on-site investigation, (2) replacing fragments of the DBMS, and (3) backing up the DBMS.

1. On-site Investigation
The on-site investigation involves doing an analysis on the original DBMS where an event of forensic interest has occurred. The on-site analysis provides the investigator with access to the DBMS without doing much preparation of an environment. Traditional live investigation practices need to be applied here and the investigator needs to be mindful not to corrupt or change the evidence. It is good practice to back up the DBMS before starting the investigation and make a copy of the log before and after the investigation to record what the investigator has done during the analysis. This approach gives the investigator quick access to potential evidence and does not require a list of tasks and specialised expertise to prepare the correct investigative environment. This method is useful when information needs to be extracted from the DBMS and the DBMS is not a suspect, but rather an impartial witness. This method may adhere to one of the criteria if care is taken and evidence is not altered.

2. Replace fragments of the DBMS
Another approach to conduct a forensic investigation of a DBMS with a found data model is to replace fragments of the DBMS installation on the suspect machine in order to realise a more trustworthy data model. In this context, replacing fragments refers to the replacing of executable files or other files that belong to the suspect data model with a similar but trusted file. If tests can be conducted to determine which part of the data model cannot be trusted, it is possible to replace that fragment of the data model with this method. Firstly, we need to determine which part of the data

model has been compromised. An md5 hash comparison between the suspect DBMS and clean DBMS may expose alterations in the data model. If a file can be linked to the data model and the replacement of the file will have no effect on the data or schema, the file can be approved for replacement. Once the investigator has found files to replace the corrupt files from a trustworthy data model, the investigator first needs to back up the current DBMS so the DBMS can be rolled back if something goes wrong. Thereafter the files can be replaced by the new clean files. If the corrupt activities of the data model can be narrowed down to a couple of files it may be easy to swap the files with clean files from the source code of the DBMS. This approach adheres to both the criteria if applied correctly. The data model can be trusted and the evidence will remain unchanged. Note that this fragment replacement method is a hybrid between achieving a clean or found data model. The live installation of the suspect DBMS is used, but the data model is cleansed by replacing fragments.

3. Backup the DBMS
It is standard practice to back up the DBMS to protect the company's revenue from a DBMS failure. When conducting a forensic investigation a situation may exist where the original DBMS has been compromised, but the backup DBMS on another machine or medium is still functioning normally and was not affected by the compromise. The original DBMS has a compromised data model that cannot be trusted which points to all our data, and the backup DBMS has a trusted data model with all the same data. When using the backup DBMS for forensic evidence it must be proved that the processes used to make the backup copy of the DBMS are just as forensically correct than making a copy of the original DBMS in a forensically correct way and taking the evidence into the lab. It should also be proved that no user edited the data on the backup server. This method adheres to one of the criteria, because we can trust the data model.

4 Data Model Forensics in Context the Other Abstract Layers of the DBMS

Problems or anomalies will almost always be detected in the lower abstract layers (like the application data and application schema) of the DBMS, because these layers are used on a daily basis and are understood by more people than the higher layers (like the source code) of the DBMS. The problem can be detected in either data results after running a query or by detecting a fault in the DBMS structures when attempting to use that structure. Some investigations might be conducted and concluded in the lower layers only, but when the attacker attempted to clear his tracks or when the output of the DBMS cannot be explained by the lower levels, the higher levels of the DBMS should be considered. This study explains how the data model can be prepared for a forensic investigation when the higher abstract layer (the data model) of the DBMS has been compromised.

5 Conclusion

Because the data model cannot be trusted to deliver correct evidence, the state of the data model should be considered when conducting a forensic investigation on a

DBMS. This paper systematically presented the methods to transform the data model into a forensically sound state. There are various forensic methods that could be used in various circumstances to conduct a data model sensitive investigation. Depending on the forensic environment, the DBMS investigator should understand the arguments for either a clean or found data model environment, and consequently select a method that is appropriate for the investigation, keeping in mind how much of the criteria the method adheres to. This study argues that no one method is adequate for every forensic investigation. The methods in this paper should be tested against a list of DBMS forensic scenarios to determine the practical feasibility of the methods. Future work includes the practical implementation of a database rootkit and an in-depth study about the rest of the abstract layers of the DBMS.

6 References

ANSI/X3/SPARC Study Group (1975), 'Data Base Management Systems: Interim Report', *ACM SIGMOD bulletin*, vol. 7, no. 2.

Beyers, HQ, Olivier, MS & Hancke, GP (2011), 'Assembling the Metadata for a Database Forensic Investigation', in *Advances in Digital Forensics: Proceedings of the 7th IFIP International Conference on Digital Forensics, 4 February 2011*, Springer, New York, ISBN: 1868-4238.

Casey, E (2010), *Handbook of Digital Forensics and Investigations*, Elsevier, California, ISBN: 978-0-12-374267-4.

Curtis Preston, W (2007), *Backup and Recovery*, O'Reilly, Sebastopol, ISBN: 0596102461.

Daniel, L (2012), *Digital Forensics for Legal Professionals: Understanding Digital Evidence from the Warrant to the Courtroom*, Elsevier, Waltham, ISBN: 159749643X.

Dyche, J 2000, *e-Data: Turning Data into Information with Data Warehousing*, Addison-Wesley, New Jersey, ISBN: 0201657805.

Greenwald, R, Stackowiak, R, Alam, M & Bhuller, M (2011), *Achieving Extreme Performance with Oracle Exadata: Best Practices for Deployments in Enterprise Datacentres*, McGraw Hill, ISBN: 0071752595.

Jakobsson, M & Ramzan, Z (2008), *Crimeware: Understanding New Attacks and Defences*. Pearson Education, Boston, ISBN: 0321501950.

Kornbrust, A (2005), *Database Rootkits*: Presented at Black Hat Europe, 29 March 2005, viewed 4 November, 2011, <http://www.red-database-security.com/whitepaper/presentations.html>

Litchfield, D, Anley, C, Heasman, J & Grindlay, B (2005), *The Database Hacker's Handbook: Defending Database Servers*, John Wiley and Sons, Indianapolis, ISBN: 0764578014.

Olivier, MS (2009), 'On Metadata Context in Database Forensics', *Digital Investigations*, vol. 5, pp. 115-123.

Overill, R, Kwan, M, Chow, K, Lai, P & Law, F (2009), 'A Cost-Effective Model for Digital Forensic Investigations', *Advances in Digital Forensics: Proceedings of the 5th Annual IFIP WG 11.9 International Conference, 28 January 2009*, Springer, New York, ISBN: 1868-4238.

Patzakis, J (2002), 'The Encase Process' in E Casey (ed.), *Handbook of Computer Crime Investigation: Forensic Tools and Technology*. Elsevier, California, ISBN: 0-12-163103-6.

Author Index

Askwith, R.	27	Katos, V.	107
		Khan, N.	76
Baier, H.	38		
Batten, L.	76	Lempereur, B.	87
Beyers, H.Q.	139		
Brand, A.	38	Mabuto, E.K.	12
		Magkos, E.	119
Cason, M.C.	66	Merabti, M.	27, 87
Chrissikopoulos, V.	119		
Chryssanthou, A.	107	Oliver, M.S.	97, 139
Fasan, O.M.	97	Pan, L.	76
		Piccinelli, M.	1
Gubian, P	1		
		Shi, Q.	27, 87
Haggerty, J.	66		
Haggerty, S.	66	Taylor, M.J.	66
Hancke, G.P.	139		
Hegarty, R	27	Valjarevic, A.	129
		Venter, H.	12, 129
Ishihara, S.	55	Vlachopoulos, K.	119